# BEYOND CENTER COURT

# BEYOND CENTER COURT

# COURT

## MY STORY

# Tracy Austin

## with Christine Brennan

WILLIAM MORROW AND COMPANY, INC.
NEW YORK

Library of Congress Cataloging-in-Publication Data

Austin, Tracy, 1962–
    Beyond center court: my story / by Tracy Austin with Christine Brennan.
        p.   cm.
    ISBN 0-688-09923-8
    1. Austin, Tracy, 1962– . 2. Tennis players—United States—Biography.
3. Women tennis players—United States—Biography. I. Brennan, Christine. II. Title.
GV994.A93A25   1992
796.342'092—dc20
[B]                                                                92-6289
                                                                      CIP

Printed in the United States of America

First Edition

1 2 3 4 5 6 7 8 9 10

BOOK DESIGN BY M. C. DE MAIO

To Mom and Dad for
your constant love
and support

# ACKNOWLEDGMENTS

I would like to thank the following people:

Pam Austin—I appreciate your being there when I began my journey inward.

Jeff Austin—Thanks for the constant special support, caring, and encouragement.

Doug Austin—Thanks for being a great brother and friend.

John Austin—Thanks for being there for me. Your emotional support has been incredible. And thanks for your awesome return of serve.

Nana—Thanks for being an incredible role model of living life to the fullest.

Tracy Tomson—I appreciate and have learned from your passion for life. You're a joy and a pleasure to know.

Kathy Johnson—Thanks for your continual insightful wisdom and knowledge.

Cari Utnehmer—Thanks for sharing, learning, and growing together over the years.

Robert Lansdorp—You've been my friend and a great coach. I couldn't have done it without you.

Sara Fornaciari—Thanks for being there like a sister when I needed you most. Your sharing and guidance helped me so much.

Christine Brennan—I cannot thank you enough for the countless hours of hard work. I treasure our newfound friendship and appreciate your hearing my voice so well.

Lisa Drew—I'm grateful to you for guidance and encouragement with this book.

Bob Shuman—Thanks for your patience and making this project fun.

Al Lowman—Thanks for your great idea. Without your persistence this book could not have become a reality.

Scott Holt—The sounding board in my life. You've made my life and my book better because of your love.

—TRACY AUSTIN

I have many people to thank for their assistance and encouragement during the planning and writing of this book. Lisa Drew of William Morrow and Company was a wonderful editor, always patient, always helpful. Bob Shuman of William Morrow offered fabulous assistance. Janet Pawson of Athletes and Artists was a great friend from start to finish—and beyond. The Austin family provided valuable anecdotes, scores, and information. And it goes without saying that were it not for the time and effort of the youngest Austin sibling, there would be no book at all. Thanks, Tracy.

Thank you to George Solomon, assistant managing editor/sports of *The Washington Post,* for giving me time off from work and constant encouragement to find new challenges. Thanks, too, to all my colleagues at *The Post* who were so kind and interested in my progress.

I was fortunate to have a wonderful group of friends encouraging me along the way, including Chris Spolar, Marty Aronoff, Tracy Kerdyk, Tony Reid, Sandy Evans and Steve Hoffman, Meredith Geisler, Mike Downey, Kristin Huckshorn, Wes Heppler, and Carolyn Mooney.

And where would I be without my family? Thank you to my parents, Kate, Tom, Jim, Amy, Randy, Brad, and Jennie.

—CHRISTINE BRENNAN

# PROLOGUE

SEPTEMBER 10, 1989
NEW YORK CITY

The Stadium Court at the National Tennis Center is one of my favorite places on earth. I won two U.S. Open titles here, the first at age sixteen in 1979, the second at eighteen in 1981. Wherever I go in life, whatever I do, it will always be the spot of my greatest triumphs, which I find rather amazing, because it all had happened before I turned twenty-one.

I go to the Open every year, and whenever I visit, my eyes dart around the place. I see the baselines, where I used to spend a fair amount of time. (Too much time, the critics said.) I see the seats in the corner where my dad and my brother Jeff sat to watch me play. I see the net, where Chris Evert gave me a pat on the head after I beat her when I was the little kid who was beginning to drive her nuts.

The nice thing about the Stadium Court is that every time I come back, it always looks the same, which means the memories are always there, waiting for me. Except for today. This stifling hot Sunday afternoon is so different. I'm not here to play tennis or commentate for television or dream about the good old days.

I'm sitting here in a wheelchair, for heaven's sake. I can't move my right leg. I was in a terrible car accident a month ago. I'm lucky to be alive.

I came to the Open as a spokesperson for Equitable, which sponsored a year-round nationwide family tennis tournament and wanted me to give out the trophies to the winners and make a speech at an awards dinner. I also wanted to watch some of the tennis, so I made my way to the wheelchair section in a corner of the court where I could watch the women's doubles.

After winning the final with Hana Mandlikova, Martina Navratilova took the microphone. I had no idea what she was about to say.

"I have a good friend here who's had some bad luck recently," she started out. "She's a former champion and actually beat me here in an emotional final a few years ago. But I know if she fights this and is as courageous as she used to be on the court, she'll be just fine. Please join me in wishing Tracy Austin good luck and a speedy recovery."

The capacity crowd applauded. Tears came to my eyes. I leaned forward, put my weight on my left foot, tried to stand, and waved toward Martina. How nice that was of her, but that's just the way she is. I came away from my six years on the circuit with a lot of good friends, one of them being Martina. People are surprised when I say that, figuring that Chris would have been a better friend of mine than Martina was, but that wasn't so. Chris and I were such rivals that sometimes there wasn't a lot of opportunity to be close friends. We were so much alike: the "girls next door" with the two-handed backhand, the tennis families, and the feminine dresses.

I was struck by Martina's kindness, but, just thinking about what she said made me so incredibly sad. You see, little more than a month before, I was planning on playing in the Open: doubles, not singles, but I was playing again, nonetheless. I was playing Team Tennis in New Jersey with my brother John, and my sights were set on the Open. I played there last year—doubles once again—losing with Ken Flach in the semifinals.

I wanted more. I had come and gone from the circuit by the time I was twenty-one, which was in 1984. I didn't "burn out," as so many people seem to think. My body just succumbed to a series of injuries to my back, legs, and foot, and I couldn't continue. It was the most devastating thing. Finished at twenty-one. To this day, even though I've moved on to a life of TV commentating, business dealings, charities, clinics, and travel, it's an unbelievable, wrenching thought. Whenever it comes up, I usually just push it out of my mind.

After dealing with dozens of doctors and physical therapists and treatments for my various ailments, I was in great shape heading into the late summer, 1989. I was dating a man in New York City, so playing in New Jersey was convenient. John, my perennial doubles partner, was making a comeback, too, limiting it just to Team Tennis. He had retired at twenty-six because of knee problems and felt that his career, like mine, was still incomplete. For me, Team Tennis seemed to be a good way to ease back into serious playing. For John, it was an end in itself.

But all my hopes ended in a split second on a gorgeous Thursday morning in early August. I was driving through an intersection when a van ran a red light and plowed into me. I don't remember much of what happened, except that when everything came to rest, I was lying on the street, my back against the pavement, my legs above me, dangling on the seat. The seat belt hung above my head, attached to the door that had flung open. My neck was killing me. My back was, too. I thought I was paralyzed.

I saw several doctors and underwent hours of X rays and exams until they figured out what was wrong with me. I was not paralyzed. My neck and back were not broken, but my right leg was, just below the knee. I ended up having it rebuilt with a bone graft from my hip and one huge screw to hold it in place. I also ended up with one long, sashlike bruise, made, thankfully, by the seat belt. There I was, Miss America!

Needless to say, I would not be playing tennis for a while—almost a year. There would be no U.S. Open for me, except in the wheelchair section.

Tennis? The U.S. Open? They weren't even priorities anymore. For three months, I couldn't go to the bathroom or take a bath by myself. I had had tennis taken away from me before, but nothing was ever this bad. And I'm not just talking about the injuries. Now, I was an adult. I had fought hard for this thing called a tennis career. I wanted it back and I wanted it badly. Before, when I was little Tracy Austin, four feet eleven inches and eighty-nine pounds, it had come and found me.

Don't get me wrong. I had worked hard for it, with the help of my parents and siblings. But this time, I had made the choice to go back. There was nothing I wanted more than a second chance at tennis.

So, as I sit here, moments after Martina has acknowledged me, replaying her words the way I used to replay points in my mind, I am struck by two thoughts:

Do I ever love this game.

And, boy, do I miss it.

# CHAPTER ONE

My mother, Jeanne, and my first coach, Vic Braden, like to tell people I won my first tennis tournament before I was born. When my mom was pregnant with me, she and Vic won a local doubles tournament in southern California. The way I look at it, they won in spite of me. My mother certainly couldn't have been very mobile.

There is no doubt, however, that I was born to play tennis. I was the last of five children in a family totally devoted to the game. For the longest time, I could beat all the girls my age, but I couldn't beat anyone in my family. That kept things in perspective for me.

My mom and my dad, George, met at UCLA when he was a captain in the Air Force and she was in her junior year. They got married, moved around the country with my dad's job in the military (he finally retired as lieutenant colonel), and had children. Pam and Jeff were born in Boston; Doug in Albuquerque; John and I in California. They moved back to California in 1956 when my dad became a nuclear physicist with TRW Inc., an aerospace engineering firm, and bought a home in Rolling Hills Estates, one of the nicer suburbs south of Los Angeles. It was to have been a temporary house, my mom told me. They still live there.

My mother never played tennis until they went back to California. Her brother, Bill Reedy, was a nationally ranked player, but she never got into the game. She grew up in Beverly Hills and her mother never thought it proper for a woman to play. Then, as a mother of four, with only me left to come along, she became a tennis nut. To get some exercise, she dragged Pam, Jeff, Doug, John, and a playpen to El Retiro Park, which consisted of two public courts. She then moved on to Redondo High School and leagues there. In 1961, she was ranked twenty-fifth in the southern California women's division. The more tournaments she played, the more people she met. One day, she was introduced to Vic Braden, a Los Angeles psychologist. Vic was a friend of Jack Kramer's, tennis champ of the 1940s, and had an idea to start a tennis club. Soon, the Jack Kramer Club in Rolling Hills was being built, Vic became the pro, and my mom began working in the pro shop. I was born two weeks before the concrete for the courts was poured, and my mom started bringing all of us kids along. Not long afterward, my mother was designing her own line of tennis dresses so she could pay for our lessons.

My dad, meanwhile, was a rocket scientist. Literally. He went to MIT and believed that education was the most important thing. He played tennis now and then, but his work in the aerospace industry and providing for us was his life. He had been poor as a child and always has had such uncomplicated, laudable goals. He rarely came to my matches, unless they were big ones, and never got involved in my tennis, unlike Messieurs Evert, Capriati, Seles, Graf, et al. He was happier if I came home with straight A's than if I won another trophy. As I look back on it now, that was just the way it should have been. I'm glad it was that way.

On the night of December 11, 1962, my mother hit balls to Pam, Jeff, Doug, and John. At six the next morning, I was born. That was how much tennis was a part of our lives.

Like most professional athletes, I began playing my sport early. Vic rolled tennis balls to me in my crib. I remember my first ball was given to me by Doug and was made of yarn. It was the only one allowed in the house. I used a sawed-off racquet and hit the ball all over the place. When I began to hit the lampshades, they moved me out of the living room. The ball still is in our house, in the frame above the sliding glass doors, where we always kept it.

My mother took me to the Kramer Club every day when she went to work and, when I was two, got me into a program for kids ages three to eight. Vic took home movies of me running around barefoot, swatting the ball with a two-handed forehand. The courts were way too big for me, so I spent most of my time on the paddle tennis courts, where everything was more my size. I've seen Vic's home movies, and I was one of the few children who seemed to know what was going on. Even at three, I had the coordination to hit the ball. Vic made tennis fun for me. He kept my friends and me running all the time. We had contests balancing balls on our racquets and counting how many balls we could pick up and put into the basket. Good strokes were not important then. He kept us running and counting and laughing. He was great at that.

I was given my first trophy at age four for hitting five balls in a row against a wall. What a feat!

"Everyone else in my family is winning trophies," I said to Del Little, the club manager. "I want one, too."

Del thought for a minute, then told me if I went to the backboard and hit five times in a row, I'd get a trophy, too. That was so important to me, I went out and hit and hit and hit until I got five consecutively. Del scratched FIVE TIMES onto a trophy and handed it to me. That little silver trophy still sits among hundreds of others at my parents' house.

Even then, I remember people focusing on me, making a big deal over me. By age three, a London tabloid had come over to take my picture and write a story about Vic and Jack's kids' program. They didn't identify me, but they printed two pictures of me with Jack Kramer's quote: "Some of them are already potential world-beaters."

At the ripe old age of four, I was on the cover of *World Tennis*. And one of our local papers, the *Daily Breeze,* ran a few photos of me that same summer. The *World Tennis* cover happened by chance. A photographer came out and snapped some pictures of Jack Kramer and his kids, and took one of me wearing navy-blue tennis shoes and a sweater over my dress. My mother jokes that had she known I was going to be featured on the cover, she would have dressed me better—or at least combed my hair.

In a way, focus on all this attention is misleading. It gives the impression that I was forced into the game, the way many young children are now by parents who are motivated by money. Nothing could be further from the truth. I loved hitting the ball then. I loved trying to keep the ball going against the backboard, and I loved running and chasing it when I missed, which was often. But I wasn't being pushed into the sport. My mother and father were interested only in my happiness as a youngster. Tennis was a diversion, just fun and games.

It sounds corny to say this, but my family was the reason I had such a good perspective. Every day, my mother picked us up from school and took us to the Kramer Club. She kept an eye on me as she worked in the pro shop and then drove us home. When I grew older, I remember I would change clothes on the way and if we came side by side with a bus or truck having a view into our car, my mom would warn me to cover up until it was safe to continue dressing. At age sixteen, we each got our own car, so we'd drive separately. At one point, there were five Volkswagens in the family.

The reason we dashed to the club after school was that there were thirteen courts at the Kramer Club and dozens of kids who wanted to play on them. There were twelve to fifteen children at my level of play alone. So, if you didn't get there early, you sat and waited.

At nights when we went home, we always set our racquets on the floor to the right of the front door. At its peak, the pile numbered thirty-five racquets. My mom would fix dinner as we did schoolwork, my dad would come home, and then we'd all sit and eat together. If I ever had a problem, there would be a half-dozen people to listen and help me at the table on any evening.

My father played tennis with me every now and then. When I was four or five years old, we would go to the local high-school tennis courts where I was hardly taller than the net. My dad remembers that people would mutter, "Yeah, sure, you're going to play tennis, ha-ha," when we walked out there. My dad loved it when those same people would stop playing and watch us as I kept the ball in play. It was his own version of *Candid Camera,* a show he loves.

"Her little feet would run down everything and she would hit two-handed shots back at me and giggle with every exertion," my dad said.

We kept up our tradition of playing together even as I grew older. I don't remember seeing my dad that much during the day; he was the typical father, leaving the house before I got up and coming home at six or seven in the evening. So, when I was ten, eleven, or twelve, I craved spending time with him. I loved hitting on the high-school courts with him and against the backboard. We weren't competitive with each other, we just liked to play for fun; my dad is the first to admit he is the worst in the family. He was the first family member I beat, which happened when I was nine or ten. But that didn't matter. I loved being out there with my dad.

He also did a good job of getting me away from tennis. On Sunday afternoons, he would take me and my friends to Space Pirate Park, an amusement center where we would spend all day on the rides, or to the Red Barn, where we would go horseback riding.

Contrary to popular belief, we were not rich. Not even close. Our house had three bedrooms—one for my parents, one for the three boys, one for Pam and me. If we had house guests—and we always did, because my mom continually volunteered to host visiting tennis players—I'd sleep on the cot in the living room. My mother always has said she got us all into tennis to keep us busy and get us out of our small house.

We had to be frugal in all kinds of ways. Even when I got older, I never had more than two half-hour lessons a week. I didn't want to become overtrained, of course, but money was the determining factor. I remember we never went out to dinner as a family, except when I was older and John and I were the only ones left in the house. Even then, it was only Sunday nights with the Fernandez family, who had tennis-playing daughters my age. Otherwise, going to Jack-in-the-Box was the big treat of the week when my father stayed late at work.

At home, we cut expenses by drinking powdered milk. Whenever I went to friends' houses and had a glass of real milk, it tasted to me like ice cream. Later on, Knudsen Dairy of Los Angeles signed me as a spokeswoman. Part of the deal was delivery of free milk, yogurt, and ice cream for our family every week. The company even bought us a freezer to store everything. No one ever knew what a treat that was.

I also loved bacon. Del Little's mother invited me over nearly every Monday to play around the geraniums in her garden and eat ice cream and bacon. I know this sounds like a bizarre combination of things to eat, but we didn't have bacon except on Christmas, because it was so expensive, and my mom really tried to stick to a budget. My Mondays were a delight—because of bacon and ice cream. My mom would drop me off as she took John to practice at UCLA, then pick me up when they were finished.

The routine varied a bit more when I turned eleven. We'd go to La Costa once a month, on a Wednesday, so John could take an hour lesson and I could have a half-hour lesson from tennis legend Pancho Segura. Pancho was known as a master strategist, so that's what we worked on. That was a special treat because we did have to watch what we spent. We weren't unusual among tennis families in that regard. Mrs. Evert was quoted as saying she found a lot of ways to prepare chicken for their family dinners.

We had to watch what we spent on clothes, too. The boys each got one pair of corduroys and one pair of jeans for the year, while Pam and I bought a couple of outfits. What made me so excited about turning pro was being able to go shopping with my school friend Cari Horn the day I got home from a tournament. I would play Martina on a Sunday and on a Monday, I would hop in Cari's little stick-shift car—she got her license earlier than I did—and off we'd go to the stores. I never bought expensive clothes, but I just loved filling my closet for the first time in my life.

Cari was a great influence for me. I met her in seventh grade and we were wonderful friends from then on. Her life was so normal; she went to all the high school dances I always missed. I would call her from a tournament and tell her how I played and she would tell me about the Friday night dance. I didn't long for that life because I loved mine, but Cari was my link to what real kids were doing.

I was five when I began semiprivate lessons with Vic, just once a week. My mom called it, "Hit, giggle, and run." But Vic said he noticed I had "excellent footwork. I like the way she bounces on her feet," he told reporters.

I started to play more in the next few years, although at age six or seven, I still wasn't playing regularly after school. I didn't learn how to keep score until one day when I was about six. I was playing at the club against Kevin Davidson, a boy who was my age. Both our moms were sitting beside the court, telling us which side—deuce or ad—to stand on. Imagine trying to explain the crazy scoring system to six year olds. We stood in the wrong spots for a while, but then we caught on.

I played my first tournament at age seven in Long Beach. All my other siblings were playing every weekend and I kept begging my mother to let me play against other kids, too. They didn't have ten-and-unders then, so I tried the twelve-and-un-ders—I was seven—and got killed by a girl named Julie Kramer, but had a lot of fun. The idea of playing made me so happy. I wore little shorts and my hair in braids, and since I had a two-handed backhand and no place to put the second ball when I was serving, I set the ball all the way back at the base of the fence. When I missed my first serve, I had to run back, pick up the second ball, and come back and serve it. Julie was a foot taller than I was, the first of many giants to face me.

I moved on to the city's age-group championships at age nine and won the 10-and-under title and the twelve-and-under title on the same day. At this time in my life, I was always playing the Fernandez twins, who are two years older than I am, in the semis and final. I always beat Anna Maria in the semis and always lost to Anna Lucia in the final. She had a huge forehand and walloped me every time, like 1 and 0.

I met the Fernandez sisters—all four of them—in the sand box at the Kramer Club. In addition to the older girls, there was another set of twins, Cecelia and Elisa, who were my age. I got into a regular routine of practicing with Anna Maria and Anna Lucia. I played Anna Maria every Thursday. On Fridays, I would play Anna Lucia, but we mostly goofed off. We made up games and dance routines and fooled around. We did this until I was fifteen or sixteen years old. We always played on an outside court so no one would spot us and get angry that we weren't practicing.

In addition to the Fernandezes, I had regular matches set up with two other girls taking lessons at the club—Trey Lewis on Tuesdays and Liz Stalder on Wednesdays. The regular schedule saved us from making phone calls and got us all into a great routine.

Despite the shenanigans on the back courts with Anna Lucia, I was serious about this game. And it showed. It turns out that my brother Jeff was predicting my success before I turned ten. He was on the men's tour and was telling his friends he had a sister who was "going to be a superstar."

They didn't believe it, but Jeff said he knew it. I've asked him how he knew and he says I had an "uncanny knack for being able to connect and whack the heck out of the ball." He said it was an "instinctive feel for how to play tennis, where to hit the ball, how to run." Not very scientific, is it? But, in the end, he was right.

Still, tennis hardly was my sole preoccupation. As I look back on it now, I really was more interested in running around with my friends than playing matches. My best little pal at the Kramer Club was Cecelia, who ended up playing collegiate tennis at USC. Beginning at age eight or nine, after I played a pro set (to eight games) on the weekend with one of the women from the club in the morning, Cecelia would come by and we would run around, playing little entrepreneurs. We'd draw pictures and sell them for one cent to some of the women around the club or we'd go to the field beside the club and pick wildflowers and put them in tennis-ball cans. Then we would take paper towels from the bathroom, draw pictures on them, and wrap them around the cans and sell the little vases for five cents. If we made seventeen cents the whole day, we were happy. We had more fun just trying to figure out ideas until one o'clock, when it was time for me to go play tennis again.

Cecelia and I looked as different as day and night: She was of Latin descent, with dark hair and dark eyes; I was a California blonde with blue eyes. But, every Halloween for five or six years in a row, we would go trick-or-treating as twins, wearing the same clothes, makeup, everything.

We were the same size—tiny. One of our favorite pranks showed how small we both were. Cecelia and I would play hide-and-seek with the other boys and girls in the boys' locker room in the dark. We both could fit into one narrow, three-foot-tall locker and we'd wait there until someone came along and tagged us. But the tagger caught only the person in front. There always was the other one in back who was never found.

They never figured out both of us were in there. I'm surprised we didn't pass out from lack of oxygen.

This wasn't my only experience sharing a small space with a friend. The first time I flew on a plane was when I was nine, going to visit Vic in San Diego, where he had moved a couple of years earlier. I was traveling with Trey Lewis, who was three years older and had flown before. I was so scared on the little propeller plane that I told Trey we had to share the same seat. The flight attendant came along, shook her head, asked someone else to move, and then tucked us into our separate seats, next to each other.

I think it's accurate to say that my childhood was as normal as the sport of tennis would allow. That's not to say my life was normal like that of a child growing up in, say, the Midwest—and sometimes I wonder what that would have been like. But, for California, and for what was going to become a big-time tennis career, it wasn't bad.

I mean, there were things like being thrown into the Kramer Club pool by my friends as a birthday ritual and hitting my head at the bottom; going up the stairs of a slide, missing a step, hitting my chin and almost biting off my tongue, which required stitches (the doctors told me I would have a speech impediment, but they were wrong); flying through our station wagon at age three when my mom stopped short for a yellow light and landing on my nose in the back of a seat, with the other four kids screaming; and being closed underneath the lifeguard stand with all the dirty laundry and only two little holes to breathe as punishment for running on the pool deck.

To sum it up, I never was far from trouble. When I was two, my mother was playing tennis with John on the court next to the pool and heard a sound. *Plop!* It was me. Otto the lifeguard pulled me out and, in the next few days, I started swimming lessons because the pool was in the center of the club and I ran around so much, I was bound to fall in again.

My diet was just as carefree. I ate three candy bars a day and drank tons of Cokes. I ruined my dinner on a daily basis. I was the queen of junk food. When a health magazine came by and asked me about my favorite snacks and vegetables, I told them the truth: "Fritos and Snickers, and I don't eat vegetables."

It's strange that I admitted that, because one rule at home was—we had to eat our vegetables.

Everyone thinks every young tennis player is very one-dimensional, which just wasn't true in my case. Until I was fourteen, I never played tennis on Monday, always taking the day off to go to Del Little's mother's house or ride horses or play on a trampoline or do something else that was fun. My mother made sure I never put in seven straight days on the court. She didn't work at the club on Mondays, so we never went there.

But the flip side was that weekends for me were not like weekends for everyone else. When I went to slumber parties, I often had to leave at ten-thirty to be ready for a tournament the next morning. I could party, but I couldn't slumber.

Even when I was at the Kramer Club, I did my best not to stand out in the crowd. I desperately wanted to be one of the gang. In fact, my peers made me a better player. There were a lot of little kids there and we all played on adjacent courts. I'd keep an eye on my friends and never wanted any of them to show me up. If another kid practiced two hours, I would practice two and a half hours.

I was very lucky to be in southern Calfornia, where we played year-round ten minutes from our house. I never moved away to a tennis camp. But even if I had not been so lucky, I doubt my parents ever would have allowed me to leave as a child, and I never would have wanted to. We never even discussed it, but, in our household, it never would have happened. Other kids have not been as lucky to have a great tennis atmosphere to grow up in and felt the need to move away.

Andrea Jaeger moved away; Jennifer Capriati moved at least two times; Monica Seles moved all the way from Yugoslavia to the United States, with her entire family in tow. It puts a lot of pressure on the child when everything revolves around her performance on the tennis court.

However, as I was growing up, I don't remember not being pointed out. At the Kramer Club, by the time I was five, I could hear people say, "Look at Tracy, how well she hits the ball." Vic Braden told people at the club, "Look at how many times she can hit the ball over the net." I was special and I was different, but I still went home for dinner at night, and my dad still came home from work, and my mom cooked in the kitchen.

I know, I know. When you're on the cover of *Sports Illustrated* at age thirteen, as I was, with the headline, A STAR IS BORN, you're anything but ordinary. But, even at that time, I was fifth-best in a family that had earned more than four hundred tournament victories at local, state, national, and international competition, including nine U.S. Tennis Association national championships. They all kept me in line. One thing I never felt was special.

About my sister and brothers: Pam always has been my glamorous big sister—thirteen years older than I am. She played on the women's circuit for nine years and always came home to the room we shared to tell me stories of France, Japan, wherever. She wallpapered our room with posters from all her travels. I remember she'd take over the kitchen by cooking weird recipes she picked up around the world. For example, she once cooked hot dogs in Coke. (I don't know what the origin of that was.) She was a night owl, staying up well past midnight with the TV going and the lights on. Meanwhile, I had to go to bed at nine for school. I quickly learned how to block out the noise and the light and go to sleep.

Pam was my idol. Her tennis dresses, her clothes, her life of travel, her boyfriends, her ways: Everything about her was so feminine. I thought she was great. I always wanted to lead the life she had. It seemed so glamorous. How ironic it is that I was the one who became ranked Number One woman player in the world, and she was the one who became a tennis director at a club in Industry Hills, California. I think she had the toughest time of anyone in my family accepting my success. If she had had another kind of career—if she had been an artist—she would not have felt so competitive with me. In fact, if we had become artists she would have been the star—because the rest of us can draw only stick figures. But her life was tennis, as was mine. When I won the U.S. Open in 1979, she never called to congratulate me.

My sister and I are opposites in many ways. She grew up tall and skinny and is six feet tall now, while I'm five feet four. She started tennis when she was around eleven; I started around two. Our own mother beat her in the semis of the women's club championship. Curry Kirkpatrick reported in *Sports Illustrated* that Pam said it was "so serious, it was awful." And he wrote that my mother never played a tournament singles match again. "I didn't like the feeling," my mom told Curry.

Pam probably would have quit the game were it not for the wonderful opportunities it provided to travel and see the world. She went to South Africa and began playing the tour there, and never stopped playing. Curry said in his article that when Pam wrote letters home, she told of Westminster Abbey or things such as funny rickshas. But when my big brother Jeff wrote, he said things like, "At 5–2, 40–30, I served to the guy's backhand and nailed him."

I will always have the largest place in my heart for Jeff, who is twelve years older than I am. When he would come home on weekends from UCLA, where he went to school and played on the team, I would run and jump into his arms. He always took time to practice with me—he'd play left-handed and always told me I could be great if I kept practicing. He also would bring me gifts, like a silver bracelet with my name inscribed on it from a tour stop in Hong Kong. (I broke it playing volleyball, but we fixed it up and I wore it until it broke again.) Even when he went to law school, Jeff came down at nights and practiced with me. He was more like a father than my father was sometimes, because my dad was so busy working. Every now and then, in big matches when I was a pro, one thought of Jeff motivated me to play better. The thought of calling him and telling him I won spurred me to more than one victory. At the 1979 Italian Open, down 4–2 to Chris Evert in the third set, I pictured calling Jeff and telling him I won. An hour later, I did exactly that. I was glad to show him all our long practices had paid off.

Jeff also played professionally, although he never thought he would. In fact, his only goal was to play at UCLA. But his game came on there, and he was ranked in the top sixty on the men's pro tour at the peak of his career, which ended in 1977. He won one tournament, in Aptos, California, in 1973. He received fifteen thousand dollars for the victory, and promptly spent it on an Alfa Romeo. Jeff is now my agent at Advantage International in Washington, D.C. He tells me that he did with his earnings what he now advises his clients never to do—spend all their money at once. He spent all his prize money in a week.

Doug is my second-oldest brother, nine years ahead of me. He is the only one not driven by tennis. He was a solid player and played at Brigham Young University and Long Beach State, but he'd rather spend time away from the Kramer Club with his buddies. BYU and Doug were not a great match; he got in trouble for kissing a girl on a date. Doug is so casual and relaxed—different from the rest of us. He was the one who wore a beard and owned one suit and two ties. And even today, he owns one suit and two ties.

The interesting thing about Doug is that losing never bothered him. He always said, "I played fine, but the other guy was better." We were worried that he might not be successful, but now he works harder than any of us and has a great construction business. He spent more time with me than anyone else in the family when I was a little girl, coloring and painting. Now he has three kids and plays with them just the way he played with me. I love spending time with them. Doug hasn't changed, and that's great.

John is five and a half years older than I am, but we ran around together every night at home and seemed much closer in age. Once, I chipped a tooth on his head playing bucking broncos. My mom always said that somebody was going to get hurt, and it wasn't going to be John. Almost every night, we would start to argue and he would warn me not to touch him. So I touched him lightly. And he hit me. On a more friendly note: We would massage each other's backs for sixty seconds. Exactly sixty seconds. To make sure it was equal, we timed it on a stopwatch.

John is an excellent player. He beat John McEnroe twice and won the NCAA doubles title at UCLA. This brings up a point: People always wonder about whether the Number One Hundred–ranked man can beat the Number One–ranked woman. The answer is yes, definitely. John was a better player than I was. The man's strength, his serve, his power, and his foot speed will dominate even the top woman player. The public thinks it's much more equal than it is. For example, when I was in my prime and practicing with John, he would hit into half the court on my side and I would have the whole court to hit back into.

He was my doubles partner most of the time and with him, I shared one of my greatest triumphs—winning the Wimbledon mixed doubles title in 1980. Things always have happened to us at the same time: His first marriage ended when I broke up with my first serious boyfriend, and, not long after I had my car accident and hurt my leg, he broke his wrist. We had a joke: If I sat on his shoulders, he could be my legs and I could be his arms, and we'd be ready to take on anyone in singles.

John now is the tennis director at PGA West in Palm

Springs. We talk all the time on the phone. If I have any kind of boyfriend problems or family troubles, he's the one I call. He's very emotional and sensitive.

All of us are still very close to one another, and it's easy to be, because we live nearby. Pam lives ten minutes from my parents, Doug lives ten minutes away, I live ten minutes away, John lives two and a half hours away, and Jeff lives across the country in Alexandria, Virginia, in suburban Washington, but comes home when he can. All in all, not bad for a family of the 1990s.

I often wonder why I was the most successful of all of us. Jeff says it was a result of several factors. "Very few people attain Number One in anything," he said. "You have to have the physical ability, the mental ability, the right environment, proper instruction, drive, focus, and concentration. Tracy was born with so many talents and she happened to be in a family environment that allowed her to thrive. If she had been born with all the same skills but had been in a family that played basketball, at five feet four inches, she would not have fit in. But all the right things came into play for Tracy. It all worked. It didn't for everyone else in the family, but by average household standards, we were pretty darn good."

There are other reasons why I became Number One. I worked so incredibly hard on my game, from hitting the ball against the backboard to playing with my friends for hours a day. I never tired of the game. I never got bored. One question I ask myself: What is it that drives people to work so hard to be successful? There is that little bit extra that some of us are willing to give and some of us aren't. Why is that? I think it's the challenge to be the best.

I always tried to be the best at everything I did, sometimes to my detriment. When I hit the ball badly in practice, I would want to hit for three hours until I got it right. This carried over to my schoolwork, too. My U.S. history teacher in high school wasn't too pleased that I missed school to play in tournaments. When I was out of town, he gave the other kids a test with twenty multiple-choice questions. When I got back, I got ten hard essay questions.

The night before the exam, I studied extra hard because I knew I was getting a more difficult test. Late at night, my mom came into my room and told me to go to bed and settle for a B. But I wouldn't stop. I did get an A—and I also got sick. That's where letting go and not pushing myself would have been the thing to do. While most children were writing chain letters, I had a clear plan of what I wanted out of life. Sometimes the mentality that got me to Number One also became my worst enemy.

Even now, I think about my boyfriend, Scott Holt. He's so easygoing. I never could be that way. I couldn't accept B's or C's. To him, those grades were acceptable, just part of a well-rounded life. And there were other reasons I became successful. My father tells a story about a time we hosted Jaime Fillol of Chile and another player at our house. I was six.

"They would play the card game Concentration with Tracy," my dad said. "That's the game where you get glimpses of which cards are where and later can capture the cards if you remember where they are. It was incredible to me and to them that Tracy was invincible. I could not beat her and they could not beat her."

My dad said I was "undisputed champ" at another card game as well. "It was 'War,' which required good hand-eye coordination. The cards are turned up from the deck and contestants grab them when one card turned up matches another. You are penalized for false moves. No one could match Tracy's reflexes. This game was hazardous to the hands and we eventually had to ban it. But she won all the time."

Back on the tennis court, Vic Braden provided a wonderful start for my budding career, because he demanded balance. He brought families to the Kramer Club, not protégés. He told *Sports Illustrated* that he was "concerned" about my "breadth early on." He said they tried to get me to play with dolls, but I'd always say no and just go on hitting tennis balls. I loved Barbie dolls, but it is true I loved tennis more than any other hobby I had.

In 1976, Vic said that things had changed. "That single-mindedness seems to have passed," Vic said when I was on the cover of *Sports Illustrated* at age thirteen. "I've always believed a young player doesn't burn herself out; the people around her burn out the youngster. Jeanne has stressed to Tracy that victories are fine, but if she stays a young lady, polite and kind, she'll always be a champion."

Curry Kirkpatrick pointed out that in 1974 at the twelve-and-under girls' nationals, I was voted "most popular" by my competitors. Jeff was quoted as saying that was incredible after I "absolutely kicked everybody's behinds, love and love."

On this subject, Vic was fabulous. He taught me a lot. I love his quote about tennis: "I wanted people to learn the joy of working hard while laughing their guts out the whole way."

Vic left the club when I was seven and was replaced by Robert Lansdorp, who became my coach through most of my career. Robert, a huge Dutchman with long, floppy hair in the style of the day, was a tough guy whom I knew loved me underneath. He should get an Academy Award for the way he acted. I wanted to kill him every day at practice—and that was exactly how he wanted me to feel.

I remember seeing him for the first time, when he came by the club to check it out, and thinking, "I want to impress this guy."

I still had a two-handed forehand. When he saw me, he said, "It's time to change." So I switched.

I found out later that Robert didn't exactly think "U.S. Open champion" when he first laid eyes on me. He told the *Los Angeles Times* in 1976:

When I first saw Tracy, I wasn't that gung ho. She was so little. I could see potential, but I wouldn't have said, "Oh, Mrs. Austin, she is going to be the greatest." It is a long process to become a champion, but gradually I saw her greatness. She learned quickly and accepted criticism. She can tell you what she did wrong without asking. I work her very hard, sometimes to the point she wonders why. But the day after a hard session she comes back and works even harder and will be disappointed if I don't push her even harder. I'm not sure whether it is because she wants to be the best or she wants to please me.

That's Robert, a real character. And that was the way he coached me. "You can't beat me . . . You can't do this, or that . . ."

"Yes I can," I said, and I showed him I could.

You often see this kind of relationship between very young athletes and their coaches. Robert became, arguably, the most important force in my life for my young tennis career. He was part father, part brother, part tyrant. The perfect coach. He worked us hard, but we also had fun. At Friday practices, all the kids would rotate in on one side of the court and, as a team, we tried to beat Robert. We played to twenty-one points and we somehow always won. (OK, he let us win.) The bet would be if we won, we got to go out for ice cream or go ice skating with him. He let us see the fun side of him.

Things started happening pretty fast for me. When I was eight, I was asked to play at an exhibition at the Newport Beach Tennis Club. I remember that John Wayne was there, playing cards. Everyone just stood and watched him play. Me included. They invited celebrities, whether they played tennis or not. I guess John Wayne just liked the atmosphere.

Then I beat Jimmy Pugh, whom I also had a huge crush on, in a mini battle of the sexes at the Forum. By the time I was nine, I frequently was asked to play exhibitions at grand openings, fund-raisers for charities, and other special events. They were great for me because they got me used to playing in front of people. In one event, I beat Rick Barry and Neal Walk, both very tall NBA players. My dad says it was funny to see me lob over them. I don't remember any scores, but I think I beat them easily.

Some of the exhibitions were cleverly staged. At the Balboa Bay Club, when I was ten, TV cameras showed Roy Emerson warming up with balls coming at him. Then the camera panned over to his opponent and showed . . . no one. The camera moved downward until it found me. I won the exhibition, but I have to admit Roy let me beat him.

Afterward, Chick Hearn, the voice of the Los Angeles Lakers, awarded the trophy. Over the public address system, he asked, "Tracy, how many trophies do you have?"

"Thirty-six," I said.

"Well, this makes thirty-seven," he said.

"No, no," I said, "I already counted this one."

At the opening ceremony for a new tennis club in Claremont, California, in 1973, Bobby Riggs played an exhibition where he took on all challengers. No one could touch him and he quickly ran out of competitors. He had it rigged so that one of the ball girls—me, then unknown—would accept the next challenge. He beat me, but I played pretty well. I was only ten and my little legs couldn't cover all the trick shots and angles he was using. Everyone patted me on the back, though, and I shrugged. Hey, maybe I really am good, I thought.

Three years later, I was to meet Riggs again. This time, I was not the ball girl. The newspaper ads headlined it SUGAR DADDY VS. TRACY AUSTIN. "Can a 13-year-old, 75-pound freckle-faced pigtailed phenom match ground-strokes with the world's self-acknowledged No. 1 male chauvinist and hustler?" the ad asked.

Our match was played before a World Team Tennis

match between the Los Angeles Strings and the Indiana Loves. By that time, I had won more than one hundred trophies. Riggs was fifty-eight and had already been beaten by Billie Jean King in their celebrated battle of the sexes in Houston in 1973. I remember watching that and thinking about how much I admired Billie Jean. Were it not for her and what she fought for in women's tennis, I could not have won the money I did. She did everything for us.

I had met Billie Jean not long before she played that match. She came to the Kramer Club to film a commercial. I had a school assignment to do a report on someone I admired. I decided to do mine on Billie Jean. I thought for sure that when I included pictures of me with her as well as her autograph to me, the teacher would be so impressed I would get an A-plus. I received an A-minus. Oh, well. . . .

Billie Jean is the most intense person I know, so driven, so focused. And she also is incredibly charming and accommodating. I kept the original of the autograph. She wrote: "To Tracy, Practice, Practice, Practice. Billie Jean King."

When I was sixteen, that autograph came back to haunt her. I played on the Federation Cup team in Madrid and Billie Jean was our captain. Her job was to make sure we got enough practice and warm-up time. Every morning, I had her on the court at eight, practicing before we played our matches. She and I laughed then that she regretted telling me to practice so much. She would rather have been sleeping.

Working with Billie Jean was great. She was a fabulous tactician as a player and a coach. She loved to study the game and its history, to work on her game as well as on others'. When I was practicing serves, she would say, "Don't pull the chain," referring to the toilets in Europe and how you flushed them by pulling down on the chain. What she meant was that on my serve, I pulled my arm down at the top of the motion. It was a wonderful analogy.

Anyway, in my match with Riggs, I broke his service twice and went up 4–0, then he came back to 4–2 before I won, 6–2. There were more than five thousand people watching at the Forum. I was a little nervous but settled down and gained confidence and had an easy time winning.

"She gets to every ball," Riggs told the reporters afterward.

A lot was made of how I looked: pigtails, braces, and a tennis dress with ice cream cones appliqued on it. I think Riggs was going to let me win, or at least make it look like that, then come back and win. But I kept hitting my groundstrokes and Riggs started huffing and puffing, and I knew I had him. Still, I was rather embarrassed by the whole thing, to the point where I covered my mouth with my hand and giggled on every point I won. My strategy back then was to play a steady game, and I figured that because he was old, maybe he'd just get tired.

At the end of the match, they gave me roses and gave him weeds.

On to the real thing. After my good results at age nine in the Los Angeles city junior events, I began winning national titles at ten when I took the indoor girls' twelve-and-under singles and doubles. I won the outdoor girls' twelve-and-under—the nationals—at age eleven and won the fourteen-and-under (indoors and out) at age twelve. I remember not having to work too hard in early-round matches. Many times they were love and love. Sometimes, I'd daydream through them.

Before I got started playing the nationals, I ran into a problem. My career was put on hold at age ten in 1973 by the strangest injury. The day I won a local junior tournament in March, Robert took a group of us from the club ice skating. I had never tried it before and my ankles sagged, so Robert, who is from Holland and skated as a kid, held my hand. I started losing my balance and he fell on top of me. I laughed—until I saw this huge bump sticking out of my leg. My right leg was broken in two places. I wound up with a huge cast from my hip to my toes and I was on crutches for three months. That was terrible. I probably could have gone to the outdoor twelve-and-under nationals that year in Little Rock, Arkansas, but I missed them. I also missed out on three months of practice. I really hated getting left behind.

The next year, when I was eleven, I won my first nationals in Savannah, defeating Kelly Henry in the finals. Kelly and I always played each other in the juniors. We were big rivals. I got to the tournament three days early to play on clay and get used to it. We don't have clay in California, but it wasn't a difficult transition. That's the tournament where I was voted most popular at the end of the week. I was totally into it. There were probably six girls who became such good friends of mine that we wrote throughout the year. It was like going to camp, only with reporters watching you.

Also that year, 1974, I was drafted for World Team Tennis. The Los Angeles Strings chose me in the twelfth round. I remember it was the first time I was mentioned in *The New York Times*—and the paper spelled my name wrong: Tracey. If the idea of an eleven-year-old being drafted to play team tennis is strange, consider that the Strings also picked Dean Martin, Jr., and Johnny Carson.

That year after my broken leg, I had some tough matches when I started to go back, but I really never lost. I won all the local tournaments, won the nationals, won the national indoors. I would go years undefeated. I lost only three games at the twelve-and-under National Public Parks Tennis championships in Arcadia, California, after my injury. For that feat, I was pictured in *Sports Illustrated*'s "Faces in the Crowd" on October 15, 1973. I moved from the last page of the magazine to the cover in less than three years.

On most of these trips, my mother did not go with me, except for the nationals, which were a big deal. The junior tournaments do a great job of matching players with families, so I stayed at local homes and got to know new people with children my age. I called my parents every day—sometimes twice or three times—but never was homesick. Even then, I loved to travel. I even loved going places by myself.

I also became resourceful for my young age. At the junior clay courts in Vero Beach, the zipper on my dress broke, so I put a sweater on and played like that during an early-round match. The problem was, it was summertime in Florida. How hot is it in Vero Beach in the summer? I nearly died.

I'll never forget that tournament because the people I stayed with had a seven-year-old daughter named Tara who was dying of a terminal illness. I fell in love with that little girl. I can't even remember the family's name now, but I believe my later interest in charity work came from getting to know Tara.

Seeing some of the best players my age made me realize how non-intense my tennis background really was. When I was at the *Seventeen* magazine tournament in Washington in 1976, I watched some little girls get up at six-thirty in the morning to jump rope and run several miles. For a couple days, I tried to keep up, but I didn't think it helped my tennis, so I told myself not to worry about them, that I was doing the right thing. Then I won the tournament.

Even with all this early success, I still considered school more important than tennis. I made all A's, read lots of books, and really didn't ever have to be told to do my homework. I was a Goody Two Shoes, I admit it. I also was different. I did miss some school time in the mid-seventies, although not very much. Just a day or two here and there for junior tournaments, and I always did my homework on planes or at the homes where I stayed. My parents wouldn't allow big trips that kept me out a week or more.

Like Chris Evert, I was treated unusually every now and then at school. One teacher put the *Sports Illustrated* cover photo of me on the bulletin board in the front of the room and kept it there all year. I didn't mind. In fact, I was proud of my achievement and was glad the teacher was, too. Most of my teachers absorbed my fame quite well. I was a good student, so I had special assignments, which included running errands for some of the teachers and helping around the classroom. One teacher even sent me to the bank, a block away. I did these things because of my work in the classroom, not because I was a tennis player.

There were some jealous kids, of course, who ran around the hallways saying I was stuck-up. I simply was very shy. That's when my friends would step in and say, "You don't even know her. Why don't you talk to her?" But that happens in every school, whether a well-known tennis player is there or not.

On rare occasions, I was made to feel rather uncomfortable. On Halloween when I was in eighth grade, my physical education teacher—Mrs. Sensenbrenner—came to school dressed as me: pigtails, pinafore dress, tennis shoes, racquet. What do you say when you see that? I smiled, but I was embarrassed. My friends teased me. I lived through it, but I didn't like it.

Tennis took me like a magic carpet to all kinds of places and all kinds of people. The best: When I was ten, a man from the Kramer Club named Bud Smith asked if I would do him a favor and play against a friend of his on Sunday. I was always looking for new people to play. Mr. Smith was a very nice man, so if he wanted me to do it, I'd do it. He told me he was going to pick me up Sunday at eleven o'clock. I asked who I'd be playing. He told me, "Some man." I had a date book—even then, I was pretty organized—and I wrote in it, "11 A.M. Sunday, Some Man."

That day, we drove up to a gorgeous house in the hills where fifty people were gathered around a private court. I didn't expect a crowd. I was in awe. And the house! I said to myself: This is the kind of mansion I hope to live in someday.

Mr. Smith introduced me to "Some Man": Laurie Belger. He was huge—six feet four inches. We went out and played, and I beat him, 6–1, 6–2. But this wasn't just another match. I found out later there were thousands of dollars riding on how I played. Laurie lost seven thousand dollars to one man and four thousand to another. He also lost four pounds during the match. He had been sandbagged. This big man never thought he could lose to a little ten-year-old girl.

That was the beginning of a wonderful friendship that lasts to this day with "Some Man." Laurie, who is married to a beautiful woman and has kids just a little bit younger than I am, started calling me "Little Poison," or "Annie." I called him "Daddy Warbucks." When I went off to Wimbledon for the first time, he bought me a necklace with a *T* hanging on it. The *T* had fourteen diamonds in it. I rarely took it off. He also bought me a diamond bracelet which I always wore during matches. Like many athletes, I had superstitions. I never took off my necklace or my bracelet when I played.

Every Valentine's Day, Laurie would send me candy. We're talking lots of candy—what seemed like twenty pounds of See's chocolate. I'd receive a tub of pralines-and-cream ice cream once a week when he found out it was my favorite flavor. He bought me four-foot chocolate bunnies and peach and strawberry pies. It was awesome.

When I was at the U.S. Open in 1977, he went to F A O Schwarz and bought a three-foot stuffed animal in honor of each player I defeated. I beat four people and have four huge stuffed animals to this day, jammed into my guest bedroom.

One time, he got tickets for me and two school friends—Suzanne DeLangis and Cari Horn—to the play *Annie*. Before we went, he and I were in Palm Springs for a tournament and he took me to a store and bought me a wonderful silk blouse and stretch red disco pants—they were in back then—and high heels. He wanted me to have fun clothes for the show. Then on the day of the show, Laurie had a limo pick up Suzanne, Cari, and me at my house. Afterward, we decided to go to Jack-in-the-Box, not because we were hungry, but because we wanted to go to a fast-food place in a limo. We giggled all the way; my friends loved coming along on my adventures, and I loved having them.

Laurie set up other matches for me against unsuspecting foes in later years and he won a lot of money from his friends. It was all in good fun. In a way, I was like his race horse, and, with me, he took his buddies to the cleaners. Laurie told me not long ago that he thinks that was the happiest time of his life. He was a very wealthy criminal lawyer, and I didn't have very much money. With all his gifts for me, he made me feel special. It was really neat to have a friend like that.

Once, a boyfriend of mine asked me when I had the most fun playing tennis.

"When I was ten," I said.

When there were no pressures, no worries. All I had were friends like Laurie Belger and dozens of matches to play.

# CHAPTER TWO

The weather was very unusual in southern California in January 1977. It was raining a lot, so my mother suggested I go with my brother Jeff to Portland, Oregon, where he had a men's professional tournament. She thought it would be good for me to play some matches in the women's tournament that was going on at the same time. I was about to participate in my first professional event, and I didn't even know it.

Over the holidays, I had won an important tournament, the Fiesta Bowl girls–eighteen–and–under championship in Tempe, Arizona. Having just turned fourteen, I upset top-seeded Trey Lewis, my almost-seatmate on my first airplane flight, in the semifinals, 3–6, 6–3, 6–1. She was seventeen and much stronger than I was. But, driven by anger, I beat her. Robert Lansdorp, my coach, was her coach, too. She was his favorite, I always thought. He would play hours with her about three times a week, which was very unusual. He also helped her more than he helped me that day. He talked to her before the match. After we split sets, we got a ten-minute break. Robert went over to Trey and sat with her for the entire ten minutes, completely ignoring me. It sounds petty now, but at the time, that really bothered me. So I beat her—and good.

A few weeks later, with no indoor courts to practice on because there are practically no indoor courts in southern California, I went up to Portland with Jeff and stayed with the Collins family, whom he was staying with and our family had known for years, and began playing in the Pacific Coast Indoor Tennis Championships. In the qualifying rounds for the event, I beat hometown girl Michelle Carey, then Belinda Thompson of England. That earned me a spot in the tournament. I vividly remember Thompson, who was seeded first. I thought she was so good and so much older than I was. How could I possibly compete with her? That was the little girl inside of me talking. The tennis player inside me said, "Kill her." And I did.

Now I had qualified for the tournament. At that time, I realized that this was more than a local event—this was a professional tour stop. My mom had said to go up there and play a match or two. She never expected me to get into the tournament. The event was called the Avon Futures, a satellite tour of the Virginia Slims, the main tour for the women pros. But, to me, it was just another tournament. Other than the papers in Portland and in Los Angeles, no one noticed or cared that I was there. Even those papers just wrote little stories. Compare that to the way Jennifer Capriati appeared on the pro circuit with such expectations and deserved acclaim.

What happened in the tournament was very interesting. From one match to the next, I kept on winning. I beat two strong college players—Mary Hamm and Paula Smith—in my first two matches. I moved to the quarterfinals and defeated nineteen-year-old future TV commentator Mary Carillo, 6–2, 6–3. The people running the tournament let me play that match a day earlier than it was scheduled for a very unusual reason: I needed to go home to go to school.

Jeff had to leave to go to the next tour stop, but my family didn't want me to be alone. So I played a day early, then flew home for two days to go to school—I was in the eighth grade at Dapplegray Intermediate School. I was missing so many classes, it was getting ridiculous, so I picked up more homework and a few fans: Robert, his wife, Susie, my mother, and my sister Pam. Pam, my mom, and I showed up on the Collinses' doorstep and they took us in. The others stayed at a nearby hotel.

I reached the semifinals by beating Mary, which, as I found out, was a big deal. The four semifinalists qualified to play in the Virginia Slims tournaments the next two weeks. So I was going to Houston and Minneapolis—if my parents and my teachers said OK.

In the semis, I played Linda Mottram of England and defeated her in three sets, 0–6, 6–2, 6–2. In the finals, I played Stacy Margolin of Beverly Hills, who was John McEnroe's girlfriend, and won when she retired from the match due to blisters on her feet in the third set, 6–7, 6–4, 4–1. It was the first time I had beaten her in three tries over our junior careers. It was a tough match and I simply outlasted her. I was beginning to get a reputation for doing that. When you play from the baseline, perseverance is everything.

The prize money for first place was twenty-eight hundred dollars, but I didn't take it because I was an amateur, and was planning to remain one for a while. Stacy, who was seventeen, a high school senior and also still an amateur, couldn't take the runner-up check of fourteen hundred dollars, either. We both were given money to cover our expenses while the prize money went back to the Women's Tennis Association.

On the court, I unwittingly had joined the big girls. Off the court, I was reminded that I was still a little kid. There were ice storms in Portland and one night before he left, Jeff, Mrs. Collins, and I got stuck at the bottom of a hill leading up to the Collinses' house. It was a clown act trying to get up the hill—I laughed so hard. We would take ten steps forward, then slide fifteen steps backward. We even tried to walk through the ivy along the road, to no avail. Finally, someone in a four-wheel drive came along and gave us a ride home half a mile away. I had to take cabs the rest of the time to the tournament because Mrs. Collins's car didn't have chains on the tires.

On the subject of Houston and Minneapolis, my parents said OK, my teachers loaded me down with homework, and off I went to Texas for the hundred-thousand-dollar Virginia Slims tournament. I remember saying good-bye to my mom at the airport and crying terribly because I didn't want to go by myself. She couldn't get away, which I understood, but it was hard on me. She arranged for me to fly alone and be picked up and taken care of by tour officials. We decided we would talk every night and see how it was going.

I was full of conflicting emotions. I was intimidated by the thought of being among the professional players, participating in their tournament, but not really being one of them. Yet, it all was very exciting to me. I was flying across the country to play with the pros—and I couldn't even drive yet.

When I got to Houston, Jeanie Brinkman, public relations director of the Slims circuit, was to keep an eye on me. Since there wasn't a family I could stay with, I stayed in her hotel room. The night before my first match, at about ten-thirty, Rosie Casals knocked on the door and popped in. I was propped up on pillows in bed in my nightgown. It was way past my bedtime, but the thought of Rosie Casals, one of the well-known veterans of our tour, hanging out with Jeanie and me, was too much to pass up. I had gotten her autograph at a tournament once. Now she was visiting my hotel room. This was great.

All of a sudden, Rosie said, "Let's order room service!"

She asked me what I wanted. I had eaten dinner hours earlier and was ready for bed, but I blurted out the only thing I could think of: "I want prime rib."

I had never had room service in my life. Prime rib sounded like the thing to order. Prime rib and a baked potato. I told Rosie to get me one of those, too.

"And what about some ice cream?" I added.

I was a twiggy little thing back then. I could eat everything I wanted. And I was about to.

We ate and talked until after midnight, when Rosie left. I had trouble sleeping that night. I felt sick from everything I had eaten.

That was the beginning of a trend; I had prime rib many nights when I traveled. What a strange thought that is now. All the players now bring pasta into the locker room; I've watched Martina Navratilova do it, and Monica Seles was eating pasta before the final of the 1991 U.S. Open. Carbohydrates are so popular now, but then, my mother's advice was to have protein. To that end, I always ate a hamburger patty before I played, even if it was in the morning. A girlfriend who had spent the night at our house laughed at me one morning when I ate meat and she had cereal. And I also ate hamburger between matches if I played two in one day. I should have been having carbos, but we didn't know that then.

My mother's words still ring in my ears: "For the third set, you need this protein."

At the time, my mom also thought it was smart for me to take salt tablets when I was playing on hot summer days. Now we know how wrong that was. The salt tablets only served to take water from my muscles to my stomach. That was exactly what I didn't want to have happen.

One morning I didn't have a hamburger was the day after my midnight binge at the Slims. Before my match that day, I did an hour-and-a-half interview with Susan Adams of *World Tennis*. She just grilled me with questions. I felt myself getting tired and my mind wandering. All this thinking, talking, and eating was getting to me.

At that time, I was only ninety pounds. Or so it said in my biography. Val Ziegenfuss, another player, read my bio in the press room and started laughing. "Ninety pounds!" she exclaimed. "No one weighs ninety pounds."

My first-round match against Linda Mottram was at six

o'clock. It had been scheduled for later, but was moved up so I wouldn't miss my bedtime. If they only knew what had happened the night before. Anyway, by the time I stepped on the court, I was fried. I was completely unprepared to play tennis and went out and lost to Linda, 6–4, 6–1. I was on the next flight home.

The next week, before I went to Minneapolis, an executive decision was made in the kitchen of a home in Rolling Hills Estates in California. Enough prime rib. Enough slumber parties. Jeanne Austin was going to Minneapolis, too.

The day the Minneapolis tournament began, I received a Western Union telegram: SO HAPPY TO SEE YOU'VE JOINED US ON THE TOUR. BEST OF LUCK ON YOUR MATCH TONIGHT. It was signed, CHRIS EVERT.

Another legend, Margaret Court, was at the tournament. It was one of the last ones she played. She was so tall and pretty quiet, but I remember that she smiled at me. I'll never forget that we saw her eating in a restaurant by herself. That was one of my few encounters with Margaret, one of the superstars of our game. As I was coming in, she was going out. I wish I had seen her play more.

I also remember that all the players loaded onto a bus to ride from the hotel to practice every day in subzero temperatures. One time, there were no seats left, so I had to sit on Olga Morozova's lap. Olga made it to the finals at Wimbledon, and there I was, sitting on her lap like a child. I definitely was out of place on the circuit—at least off the court. There were no other young kids on tour. At night, if I didn't have a match, I would do my homework and other players would go out together or on dates.

I won my first-round match against Greer Stevens, the Number-One player from South Africa, 7–5, 6–3. Greer was half a foot taller than I was and a very good player. For my first Slims victory, I could have received $1,375, but I turned it down to remain an amateur. At that time, I was thinking I wouldn't turn pro until I was eighteen. Things happened much faster than I ever anticipated. I gave up my amateur status just a year and a half later, when I still was fifteen.

In the second round, I lost to Rosie, 6–3, 6–3; at twenty-eight, she was twice my age. She drop-shot, lobbed, and volleyed me to death.

I was asked to go on to the next tour stop in Seattle, but my mother and I headed home instead. My mom explained why, when she spoke with a reporter for the *Minneapolis Star:* "We don't think Tracy should extend herself at this level right now. I think it's time for her to go back home, to go back to school, to put a little normalcy back into her life."

My mom said that if I had enough Virginia Slims points to qualify for the Los Angeles tournament in February, I could play. "Otherwise," she said, "I think this experience has been enough for a while."

Imagine one of the tennis mothers of the nineties saying that.

I found out two things those first two weeks on the Slims circuit: I was too young to take care of myself; and I wasn't yet good enough to play great tennis against the big names. So I have to laugh when I look back at some of the newspaper clippings from back then. *The New York Times* wrote that I displayed "tremendous maturity" and projected "a confident quality" when I spoke. "While watching one of the more experienced players practice last week, she was advised by a companion to notice the strength of the player's forehand. 'I don't think her forehand looks so great,' she said. . . ." That was from *The Times.*

I was just being honest. I didn't look at it as confidence then. On the court, I felt twenty-five. Put me at 4-all in the third set and I could handle it. But put me in a conversation with the other players in the locker room and I would do a lot of listening.

Even so, at fourteen, I was physically much weaker than the other girls and women I was playing. Compare that to Jennifer Capriati now. She is their size—or bigger. Even Rosie

Casals was small, but she was a serve-and-volley player and I couldn't stay in there with her. I was overpowered by her.

I came home and played another junior tournament— and won it. Then I went to the Los Angeles Slims event at the Sports Arena and again lost to Rosie in the second round, 6–4, 6–4. (I was gaining on her, though.) By now, I was in the lead paragraph or headline of most newspaper stories. They called me "the talk of tennis," "the new Chris Evert," you name it. At first glance, I did appear to be the new Chris, what with the pigtails and two-handed backhand and the tennis-playing family. But I grew up on hard courts while Chris played on clay in Florida, and I think that made me more aggressive. On the court. Off it, I was shy and self-protective, like Chris was when she came out on tour.

I was known in interview rooms for yes-and-no answers. This came back to haunt me when I interviewed Jennifer at the U.S. Open in 1991 for USA Network. I asked these wonderful, thought-provoking questions, and she came up mostly with a *yes* or a *no*. It really left me hanging on live TV, but it was totally appropriate for someone her age.

This brings up something that bugs me to this day: the way a few people perceived my image. I had pigtails even when I was sixteen years old. I was so naive. Kids today are wearing strapless dresses at age fourteen. I remember JoAnne Russell saying that I wore the pinafores and pigtails for effect, that my mom dressed me that way for some kind of psychological advantage. She suggested that I overdid the "young, helpless look." She said I did it to make myself seem so little, which then would allow me to catch everyone by surprise.

That's just plain wrong, and it really hurt me. I *was* just a kid. Didn't anyone understand that? JoAnne was being nasty because she was losing to me. I beat her twice in a row within two weeks, so she lashed out. But winning wasn't everything. Little did people like her know how sensitive I was.

During the rest of the 1977 season, I would do something girls never do now: I would play a pro event, then go back and play an age-group junior tournament, where I never lost. I'm not being arrogant; it's just true. At that point in my career, I had never lost to someone my age. So I'd get that pro experience, then play in the juniors and get my confidence back. For example, I won the girls' eighteen-and-under in Port Washington, New York, in February and played it between two pro events—the Virginia Slims of Los Angeles and the Family Circle Cup, where I had my first really big upset of a professional when I defeated Dianne Fromholtz, 7–5, 6–4, in the second round.

That victory over Dianne at Hilton Head in March was interesting. She was the sixth-ranked woman in the world and had been to the semis of the U.S. Open the year before. Dianne was one of the nicest women on the circuit. She never made me feel uncomfortable. She became a good friend and a practice partner of mine in Los Angeles. That day, we played on clay, an unusual surface for me, so it was an especially good win for me. Afterward, I was thrilled. I couldn't believe I won. Nor could Dianne. "How can anyone so young be so good?" Dianne said at her press conference. "I took her too lightly."

I lost in the quarters to Kerry Reid, 6–3, 7–5. Again, I just don't think I was strong enough yet to win. Kerry dropshot me and lobbed me and simply overpowered me with a huge forehand. It was like she had me on a string. She was just too much. So I went back and played the girls' 18s and felt good about myself again.

Living in this serious world, I was adept at providing distractions for myself. At the Hilton Head banquet, a magician moved from table to table, performing tricks. He dropped an orange onto one of the tables and then came up with it underneath, as though it had gone through the wood.

This puzzled and bugged me, so when the magician moved on, I followed him, by myself. I'd love to say a group of kids went with me, but there were no other kids. I wanted to sneak up on the guy and find out if he had secret holes in the tables. I never found out—but I tried.

The magician intrigued me. So did golf carts. I loved them. I couldn't drive a car, but I could drive a golf cart, and most tournaments allowed me to use one around the grounds. Once, Bettina Bunge and I were driving a little too fast and nearly tipped over. Another time, when I arrived at a tournament in Florida after the 1979 U.S. Open, I found a special golf cart waiting for me. It had a sign on the side: U.S. OPEN CHAMPION.

But, in 1977, I had not been to a U.S. Open yet, or Wimbledon. At every press conference, reporters would say, "What about Wimbledon?"

Honestly—and I know this sounds odd—I *didn't* know. I was hoping to go, but I was under the impression I had to be sixteen to be eligible for the main draw. Then Wimbledon officials told the press I was old enough and they were sending me an entry blank. My mother kept telling reporters it was premature to discuss it, probably because she knew if I started thinking about Wimbledon in March and April, I wouldn't concentrate as I should on school and my other tournaments.

But as we got closer, it became clearer that I was going to go. It was the one-hundredth-anniversary tournament and I was going to be the youngest person to compete there since 1887, when a thirteen-year-old named Lottie Dod played. You don't think the London tabloids cared much about that, do you?

The flashbulbs popped in my face the moment Robert, Susie, my mother, and I stepped off the plane. Twenty reporters were there—and it was six-thirty in the morning. I didn't know reporters got up that early. I never thought there would be that much interest in me. Never.

I first played in the Wimbledon warm-up in Edinburgh, Scotland, to get used to grass, which wasn't exactly my favorite surface, since I had played on it only once, at the girls 18s the year before. I lost in the second qualifying round in Edinburgh, but I felt good.

On to Wimbledon. My father met us there, and he arrived with a bizarre story. He had flown into Gatwick, not

Heathrow, and then had to take a one-hour train ride to Victoria Station. He hailed a cab to take him to the Gloucester Hotel, where the players were staying. During all this time, he talked to no one—not a soul at Gatwick, on the train, at the station. He hopped into a cab and the driver struck up a conversation.

"That fourteen-year-old miss is quite a sensation," the driver said right off the bat.

My dad said later he was stunned. He had traveled five thousand miles and the first person he talked to immediately brought up his very own daughter. But my father, never one to bask in the limelight, didn't say who he was. The cabbie launched into a discussion that I was too young to be playing Wimbledon, that I should be home like other fourteen-year-old girls. My dad never said a word, but the driver was a bit embarrassed when he pulled my father's luggage out of the car and caught a glimpse of the baggage tag. We all got a good laugh from that.

I was Alice in Wonderland in the days leading up to Wimbledon. In the hotel lobby, Arthur Ashe came over to say hello. I had never met him before and I was so amazed he knew me that I could only stand there with my mouth open, saying nothing. My sister, who also came to watch me play, pointed out Ilie Nastase in the lobby and I met him, too.

Actually, we had met once before, but I hoped he didn't remember. I was ball girl for Ilie and Jimmy Connors when they were playing doubles at the Los Angeles Tennis Club when I was ten. Before the match, you're reminded to go and get the serve when they hit it into the net. One time, they were in the middle of the point when there was a let-cord and the ball bounced toward me. Instinctively, I went out and grabbed it and went back to my place. Unfortunately, this occurred in the middle of a point. Ilie gave me a tremendous staredown and I thought I was going to cry. I was so nervous. All I wanted to do was the right thing. They replayed the point and I somehow recovered. My ball-girl career was over, however.

It was John McEnroe's first Wimbledon, too. (He reached the semis.) He was almost four years older than I. The photographers wanted a picture of the two of us at the Wimbledon Ball, which then was held on the middle Sunday of the tournament. I've always felt John and I have a bond because we both came into the public eye in a huge way at that tournament. To tell the truth, we both were overwhelmed by all the attention.

I first saw the beautiful, old grounds of the All-England Club through a hole in the fence, like a tourist. A BBC driver took me by the stadium and the grounds after an interview, and it was locked, so I sneaked a peek and thought it looked just as I had imagined: ivy on the walls, big flowers everywhere. Even then, I was struck by the tradition of the place. I knew what it meant. I had read up on it in tennis books. I knew some of the names of the winners from years past; that was important to me.

When I got inside, it was even better than I had hoped it would be. The champions' names were painted on the walls. It was a beautiful green, not sterile at all, and smelled and felt like history.

The British tabloids quoted me as saying, "It holds no terror for me," which was made up, because I never talked that way. They often put their words in your quotes, which was something that took some getting used to. I do know this; I was in awe privately, but, publicly, I was fearless.

The day before Wimbledon began, I practiced at the staid Hurlingham Club to get in more experience on grass. They didn't allow you to practice at Wimbledon or any other club on Sundays. The fans stood five-deep watching me. That surprised me. I had never seen anything like that before. The weather that day was the usual cold and damp; I wore my winter coat at the garden party at the club, a photographer snapped some pictures of me, and that photo made the rounds in the next day's papers. The press had been amazing. They asked me so many insignificant questions: if I had my ears pierced (yes); if other players liked me (I thought so); and what I thought of Idi Amin (who cares?).

I had a bye the first round and faced Elly Vessies-Appel of the Netherlands on June 22 in my first match on Court Seven, one of the outer courts. I won easily, 6–3, 6–3, despite some early nerves. I remember it was a crisp, sunny day and I wore a white dress with a big bow in the back and a pocket in front, where I always instinctively put a tennis ball. The dresses were made by a company called Little Miss Tennis. The woman who started the company had a daughter who played nationally. She never knew where to put the ball either, so her mother designed a pocket for her. I met the woman at the 14 nationals and she gave me a few dresses on the spot. They were so comfortable and loose, I wore them to death. I soon received a limitless supply.

I remember that Elly was nearly a foot taller than I was, which made for funny pictures of us shaking hands. I also remember my mother crying when it was over, but I think that was because she's allergic to grass, not because she's emotional. That's a problem for some of the players as well. Tennis players who are allergic to grass get shots all year in order to build up their resistance when Wimbledon comes around.

The victory over Elly set up the biggest match of my life to that point. On Friday, June 24, I played Chris Evert for the first time ever. The buildup for the match was incredible. It began when the draw came out and everyone saw we could meet in the third round. She was the defending champion. I had become the focus of every tabloid in town. The reporters couldn't get enough of it. They were billing it "the looking-glass war," because of our similar styles of play. I can't imagine the pressure Chris was feeling that day. She was being asked about me regularly, and, gracious as always, she said very nice things. I read one of her quotes that said there was no way yet to know how good I was. "We'll know by the time she is 17. By 17 or 18, if you haven't broken into the top three, you never will." She was correct then, and she is correct now. It's almost more of a girl's game than a woman's.

I felt no pressure. I had nothing to lose. In fact, I was more nervous about curtsying to the royal box than about playing.

So there I was, fourteen, facing Chris on Centre Court in front of fourteen thousand fans on a bright afternoon. I had played exactly four professional tournaments and had won a grand total of twelve thousand dollars, which I had given back. I had won 128 tournaments as a junior, and was to win some more. Chris, well, was Chris, the top-ranked player in the world, and the person I was most like. In her autobiography, she wrote that she got sick to her stomach before we played. Chris must have spent an hour in the locker room putting on makeup: bright-red lipstick, mascara, everything, all just to go out and play tennis. Her nails were perfect. She wore a sun dress that accentuated her bust line. I mean, her boobs were just hanging out. I didn't have that problem yet.

She put on a necklace that read BABE, a gift from Burt Reynolds. She was twenty-two and dating and into guys and all grown up—it seemed to me. I was fourteen and, as Bud Collins wrote in *The Boston Globe,* looked like "a deserter from the Campfire Girls." He was right.

We got ready in separate locker rooms. I was downstairs in the bowels of the stadium in a dungeon with no windows. She was in the seeded-players' locker room, which is much nicer. It's like a lounge with windows that overlook the far courts. There were couches with floral prints and everyone had their own bath cubicle. A pleasant lady named Mrs. Frazier was there to help the sixteen-or-so players. She washed the players' clothes and set out afternoon tea and biscuits. There was a hair stylist up there, too.

They called me and said to meet Chris in the Centre Court waiting room. We were there for just a minute or so;

officials just want to make sure they know where you are so you're ready when the TV people want you to come out. In the room, Chris told me how and when to curtsy to the royal box. We walked out onto the court together, warmed up, and started playing.

I won the first game at 30, then Chris came back to 1–1. In the third game, Chris slipped and fell chasing a ball, landing on her butt. She was so embarrassed. At the time she was ultrafeminine, unlike her later years, when she became more proud to be an athlete, spills and all. Chris said she heard the clicks of a hundred cameras and, sure enough, that was the photo all the papers used the next day. Newspapers love it when you look stupid.

From then on, it wasn't much of a match. Chris won, 6–1, 6–1, in a total of fifty minutes, and although I thought she was on her way to a third Wimbledon title, she ended up losing in the semis to eventual champion Virginia Wade. But I played well and was proud of myself. My family had been worried I might turn into a zombie and not be able to do anything. On the contrary, I had come out with my reputation not only intact, but enhanced. Chris said it was the toughest match emotionally of her career. I felt instant respect from her. What's more, Chris had not played at Wimbledon until she was seventeen; I was three years ahead of her.

The whole Wimbledon experience was a whirlwind I'll never forget. Billie Jean King suggested to me that I write down my feelings as my first Wimbledon went along. I thought that was a good idea, but didn't follow up on it until a few years later, when Sara Kleppinger Forniciari, my agent from ProServ who traveled with me, gave me a diary for my sixteenth birthday. I have kept one, off and on, ever since. Sara encouraged me to write down what I was going through so I could appreciate it later, and, while I don't go back and read them very often, I love the thought that those diaries are sitting on a shelf in my office, in case I want to leaf through them.

If I had kept a diary then, I probably would have written

about several things. I remember going to the tearoom every chance I got to see what famous players were there. From the tearoom, which was filled with wicker chairs and floral pillows, I would go up on the roof and get a great view of all the outer courts. It was fun. And, oh yes, I loved the strawberries.

I turned down the chance to dance at the Wimbledon Ball with Jean Borotra, a tall Frenchman who was one of the famed "Four Musketeers" of French tennis in the twenties. He was the oldest person at Wimbledon and I was the youngest player. But I was too shy and didn't want to slow-dance in front of people.

The rest of my summer was a series of age-group tournaments with a couple losses to Martina Navratilova at two Slims tournaments mixed in. I was upset by Linda Siegel in the semis at the girls 16s in Charleston, West Virginia, but otherwise won everything in the juniors. Linda played very well to beat me, but this showed how difficult it was for me to live up to everyone's great expectations. I was feeling tremendous pressure playing against the pros and then coming back to the juniors. I put too much pressure on myself against Linda.

I called my dad on the phone after the match. "I'm just so sick of losing," I told him. One loss and I was sick of it. I imagine that's why I barely ever let myself lose.

In the 18s, I beat Kathy Jordan for the title. I felt great. I was back on track in the juniors. Pretty soon, I was headed straight for my second Grand Slam event—the U.S. Open—and another big step in my fledgling career.

I made it all the way to the quarterfinals in the last year the Open was held at the West Side Tennis Club in Forest Hills. Although my greatest triumphs were to come when the Open moved to Flushing Meadows, I loved the old Forest Hills courts. There was no parking garage there; you parked your car on the street and walked as if it were a weekend match at the local club. Forest Hills to me represented legendary courts and intimacy and tradition. Even at my young age,

I appreciated the beauty and the history of the place. It was like no other club in the United States I had been to except for the old Philadelphia clubs.

I beat Heidi Eisterlehner of West Germany in the first round and Donna Ganz of Miami in the second before meeting Sue Barker of England, the fourth-ranked woman in the world, in the third round. It took fifty-nine minutes for me to beat her, 6–1, 6–4. The pressure I put on and my consistency won the match. It was so easy, it never dawned on me how good she was. Sometimes, you go on autopilot. It's better not to think. Believe me, I was just running on raw talent back then.

My brothers Jeff and John were playing doubles at the same time. We had hoped my match would go on before theirs, but it didn't, so they told me they strained to hear the public-address announcer say my scores. It was Jeff's last tournament before he went to law school at UCLA. He already had quit the tour but decided to play with John because John was just coming up and Jeff wanted to help him along.

In the fourth round, I played Virginia Ruzici of Romania in the Stadium Court with more than twelve thousand people watching. I defeated her 6–3, 7–5, to become the youngest quarterfinalist in Open history.

I guess I was making quite an impression because I received a phone call from President Carter after beating Virginia. The call came to the locker room and a woman handed me the phone, saying it was Jimmy Carter wanting to speak with me. I didn't believe her. How many times do people joke about things like that? Well, this time, it was true. My conversation with the President went so fast, I don't remember what he said, except something about playing really well and if I ever came to Washington, I could be his guest at the White House. I think I said I would take him up on it. I don't really remember saying much. I was stunned. I finally did make it to the White House to give his daughter, Amy, my racquet when I won the Open in 1979.

Two days later, on September 7, 1977, I was playing six-feet-one Betty Stove of the Netherlands (why did I always get these tall opponents?) in the quarters. I lost, 6–2, 6–2. Betty, the Number Five seed and Wimbledon runner-up, killed me, sometimes pushing me back fifteen feet behind the baseline trying to return her shots. She was just the type of player I could not handle back then. Her power was too much for me. Robert Lansdorp said Betty must have been playing on Mars. She was out of this world, she was playing so well. I might as well have been on Pluto. She was so strong she had me back on my heels for all of the fifty-six minutes we played.

The next week, I went back to school for my freshman year at Rolling Hills High. This was a big day for me: my first day of high school. My brother John showed me around the school a few days before and I felt so intimidated. The place was huge. I was worried because my best friends, Suzanne and Cari, were going to other high schools and I didn't know anyone. I stuck out because of my fame and I was brutally shy on top of that. It was very hard for me until I found some new friends.

When everyone told what they did on their summer vacation, well, I had a lot to say. My hometown had "Tracy Austin Day." Agents were calling. Endorsements were mounting. Offers were coming from everywhere. A tournament in Japan called and wanted me to come and play, meaning I would miss the beginning of school. I said no. I had had enough for the moment. But there was no doubt I was waking up to a new, wonderful world. There were opportunities galore for me. Translated, that means agents.

My parents were in charge of this area of my life and I remember they asked Jack Kramer for his advice. Jack suggested Donald Dell, the former player who ran ProServ, the Washington-based sports marketing and management firm. Sara Kleppinger (she later became Forniciari) and Donald came out to the Kramer Club to meet me, and I liked them, but I really didn't care when they discussed business. International

Management Group, Mark McCormack's company in Cleveland, sent Bob Kain, one of their representatives. There were dozens of others who called or came by the house. We lived close to Hollywood, after all. But I didn't pay much attention to any of them. I knew this was something I would have to deal with, but I didn't really want to. When they came over, my parents would talk to them and I would go to my room and do my Spanish homework.

Soon, my parents agreed to let Sara and ProServ become my unofficial adviser from late 1977 through 1978. She worked on a pro bono basis, just to help me and my family get adjusted to this new side of my life. It was good for us and good for ProServ, too, because they got the inside track in working with me. Of course, when I signed with them, this was business, but, with Sara, it was more than that. She would come by to see me and my mother and would call often. She was Jeff's age, so I found I could relate to her as a big sister. When I signed with ProServ, she traveled with me off and on, roomed with me occasionally on the road, and became one of my best friends—and remains so even now. Although Sara no longer represents me and now has left ProServ to form her own company, I call her often—as a friend.

I was learning all kinds of things at this time in my life. I watched transsexual Renée Richards undress right before me in the bathroom at the Port Washington Tennis Academy. This requires some explanation. I was playing a junior tournament there, which coincided with the Lionel Cup, a tour that my sister directed. Renée Richards was playing on that tour. I was there on a Sunday afternoon and went to the bathroom with a friend. Renée then walked in. Obviously, I knew who she was and she knew who I was. We started talking about the tour and when Pam was coming into town. All the while, she was undressing and I was beginning to feel a little uncomfortable. Perhaps she felt she should just act normally and undress in the women's room, although maybe she should have been more

sensitive. I wanted to finish the conversation and get out of
there.

Because of the controversy concerning Renée on the
women's circuit, my mother and I had to go to Lenox Hill
Hospital when I was at the Open as did all female players so
I could be medically proved to be a woman. The sex test took
a second—just a little scraping of tissue inside the mouth. But
what I remember most is the giggles we had over it. My mom
went up to the nurses and said, "We have to prove my daughter's a girl."

I began to have to deal with new issues. When I went to
Portland earlier in the year, a girl who was four years older
than I was started talking about some woman's girlfriend. I
said, yeah, I have girlfriends, too. No, this girl kept saying,
this was different. That was how I learned what a lesbian is.
It's an issue on the circuit, but not a big one. I didn't worry
about it and it's never bothered me.

A few years later, when John and I were in Japan to do a
promotion for Gunze, the clothing company we represented
in the United States, the officers of the company thought it
would be so wonderful to take us to a transvestite show. A
little uneasy, we went along with their plan. Well, we got there
and there were men dressed as women and I have to say they
were absolutely beautiful. We were laughing so hard that I
think we embarrassed the men from the company. John is six-
feet-three and I'm a blonde, so we stuck out like sore thumbs.
We went backstage after the show and met the men . . .
women . . . whatever you want to call them.

In Stuttgart, at age fifteen, I was taken to another transvestite show. I was becoming a regular at it. There was a fat
guy, about four hundred pounds, dressed up as "Heidi."
When he would lift his arms, you saw all these warts and everything. It was so disgusting. See what a glamorous life I was
leading?

I was so incredibly innocent back then. I didn't know
anything about drugs, cocaine, people sleeping together, and

any other alternative life-styles California has made famous. Even when I had boyfriends and was exposed to college life, as when I dated tennis player Matt Anger from USC, I never saw any of that stuff. I have never tried drugs of any kind, marijuana, anything. I imagine it's all out there on the tennis tour, but I was so young—and so sheltered by my mother, family, and friends—that I never did any of it. People often ask me about drugs on tour. Maybe I'm naive, but I never knew who did what—or if anyone did anything at all. I assume players were experimenting with marijuana, but I don't know who or when or where. I wasn't invited to those parties, if they were happening at all. And I'm very glad I wasn't.

I found out a few years ago about a rumor that I had come off the circuit at such a young age because I had a cocaine problem and had to go to a rehabilitation center. Scott Holt, the man I date now, had heard this rumor before we met. On our third date, Scott asked me if I ever had tried drugs.

"No," I said.

"I see," he said. "Strong denial."

"What?"

I told him it just wasn't true. Scott later mentioned the name of the friend who had told that story. Months later, I met the man at a party. I didn't miss my chance.

"Why are you telling a story like that?" I said. "It's wrong and it's terribly unfair."

He was so embarrassed he wanted to dive under a table. I was so glad I confronted him. When you hear a rumor like that, it makes you wonder what other false stories are out there circulating about you—and about others.

Here's one I found out about. Someone also told Scott that I had breast implants in Newport Beach. For starters, I don't know any doctors in Newport Beach. And, much more significantly, if anyone's ever seen me in a bathing suit, they would know that whoever did this mythical surgery would have been out of business the next day.

LEFT: Three years old. What a sexy outfit! I was always barefoot—getting shoes on me was a tough task.

BELOW: Bend your knees, watch the ball, and follow through. I still make funny faces today when I hit the ball. Pretty good form for a three-year-old!

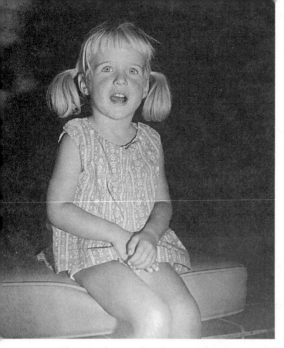

THE WORLD'S LARGEST TENNIS MAGAZINE
JULY 1967
60¢

world/tennis

The pigtails started early. I was four here, at the Jack Kramer Tennis Club, where I spent most of my days because my mom worked there six days a week.

My first magazine cover at four years old in 1967. My mom said that if she'd known, she would have dressed me better and combed my hair! PHOTOGRAPH BY DAVID POWELL, *World Tennis*

On the steps of the Kramer Club in 1966 with my whole family. *From left*: Jeff, me, Mom, Pam, Dad, John, and Doug.

# How a champ is born at the age of THREE

IS IT any wonder that Wimbledon, the pinnacle of Britain's tennis year, has sometimes looked more like an American trophy-collecting convention?

This could be one of the reasons. Catch them young is accepted sporting doctrine. In America it is accepted practice.

Jack Kramer, king of the professional tennis circuit, and Los Angeles psychologist Vic Braden have opened a school in California.

Their pupils are three and four years old. Their aim: To keep America on top of the tennis world.

## Emotions

At a recent children's tournament, Kramer pupils took most of the prizes. Kramer predicts: "Some of them are already potential world-beaters."

His philosophy is simple: "Children are not given enough credit for physical skills," he says. "Just let them hold a racquet and they'll think. Thinking means growth, development."

But Kramer admits that young losers can show the emotions anyone would expect.

Sometimes they throw a tantrum and they have even been known to kick the ball or stick their tongues out at their opponents.

First Kramer tells a pupil how to do it . . .

. . . then she swings two-handed—and it's lesson accomplished

The London *Daily Mail* did a story on Jack Kramer and just happened to use my picture. Little did we know then that I would use the Jack Kramer autograph racket to win the Open thirteen years later.     LONDON *Daily Mail*

BELOW LEFT: At seven, winning my first trophy. I think I liked this thing called winning!

RIGHT: With my first coach, Vic Braden (*left*), and tennis great Jack Kramer. They started the club where I grew up and made tennis fun from the beginning.     PHOTOGRAPH COURTESY OF MELODY BRADEN

ABOVE: With Karen Bunag (*to my right*), Kelly Henry (*to her right*), and Suzy Jaeger (*to my left, in pigtails*) at the 12 Nationals in Savannah, Georgia. We played cards every second we got. I was voted most popular.

LEFT: My first *Sports Illustrated* cover at thirteen. The story inside was about our whole family. I hated those braces!
PHOTOGRAPH BY JOHN G. ZIMMERMAN, *Sports Illustrated*

ABOVE: Sitting for our 1976 *Sports Illustrated* portrait. *From left*: Doug, Jeff, Dad, me, Mom, Pam, and John. This is our family room with all of our trophies. The shelves started out with books, which eventually had to be replaced.     *Sports Illustrated*

BELOW LEFT: Playing Wightman Cup at the Royal Albert Hall in London in 1978. Billie Jean King, Chris Evert, and Pam Shriver were on the team. Ted Tinling made me the dress with American flags on it. RIGHT: Playing Wimbledon in 1978, where the clothing has to be 90 percent white. Ted Tinling made all my dresses and special white ones for Wimbledon.

ABOVE: After beating Chris Evert 6–4, 6–3 to win the U.S. Open in 1979. Can you guess who won?
PHOTOGRAPH BY CAROL L. NEWSOM

LEFT: The *Sports Illustrated* cover the week following my Open victory over Chris. She had won it four years in a row. I was in shock!   *Sports Illustrated*

My brother John and me at the beginning of the Wimbledon mixed doubles finals. At that time matches *never* started before 2 P.M., but because of rain we were pushed back to the final Sunday. We started at 12 P.M., right before the incredible final between John McEnroe and Bjorn Borg.     PHOTOGRAPH COURTESY OF JOHN AUSTIN

BELOW LEFT: The winning moment! RIGHT: We never even dreamed we could win the Wimbledon mixed doubles in 1980. We are the only brother-sister team to win Wimbledon.

PHOTOGRAPHS BY CAROL L. NEWSOM

The victory dance. I can't believe it! I had just beaten Martina Navratilova, 1–6, 6–1, 7–6, to win the U.S. Open in 1981.
PHOTOGRAPHS BY CAROL L. NEWSOM

LEFT: Looking back at my dad and brother. My mom and coach Marty Riessen were sitting in the same lucky seats they had sat in all two weeks—at the other end of the court.
PHOTOGRAPH BY CAROL L. NEWSOM

# CHAPTER THREE

I turned professional on October 23, 1978, less than two months before my sixteenth birthday. Jim Murray of the *Los Angeles Times,* one of the best sportswriters in the country, wrote a very unflattering article about me in the paper the next day. How awful it was, he said, that I was going to be traveling around the world at such a young age, staying in hotels, missing the prom, leading such an abnormal life. It really made an impression on me because Jim Murray was always my dad's favorite writer. At the press conference, I was incredibly bubbly and gushed that he was my dad's favorite. I was thrilled he was there to see me. Then I woke up and opened the paper and he ripped my decision up one side and down the other.

I ran into Jim Murray again when we sat next to each other at a charity dinner in Los Angeles. My date was a baseball player who was with the New York Mets and he and Jim got into a great discussion about the sport. Jim really knows his stuff, plus he is a warm and sweet man. I found him fascinating, even if he didn't like my career choice. Having that kind of experience with Jim's column made me wary of the press right away. I was just fifteen and quite sensitive. I learned quickly that it was best not to read the papers, which is hard, because you're curious about what everybody else is reading about you. I also learned never to believe what you read about yourself. Joe Paterno, the Penn State football coach, says if you start to believe what they write about you, you're in big trouble. My mother had her own theory: "Never read what they write about you because if it's good, you'll get a big head and if it's bad, your feelings will be hurt."

To back up for a moment, after the 1977 Open, I moved back to the age-group competition and won it all. When I would make the occasional foray into Virginia Slims tournaments, I would win a round or two, then lose to Virginia Wade or Martina Navratilova. Now fifteen, I had grown three inches since the summer to five feet two inches and had gained eight pounds to reach ninety-eight. I was even getting seeded in Slims events. When I lost to Martina at the Los Angeles Slims tournament in January 1978, I was seeded eighth. Martina, seeded Number Two, beat me, 6–3, 6–4 in the quarters. It was the third time she had defeated me in three matches; the first two were immediately before and after the U.S. Open in 1977.

Afterward, Martina said at a press conference that she had everything to lose and I still had nothing to lose. "Can you imagine the headlines if I lost?" Martina asked. "I realized that before the match. Here I am being beaten by a fifteen-year-old. Tracy makes us all feel like old ladies."

Combine that with JoAnne Russell's comments that I was faking them all out by dressing like a little girl and you can see that they all loved me out there. But, in their defense, I should say it must have been hard for them to accept me. I was a threat to them. Eventually, I started to build my own friendships, but it was tough at first. I read that Chris said she felt that way, too, when she first arrived on the circuit. I really wasn't made to feel all that welcome and it probably made me want to beat them even more. They didn't know how to react to a fourteen-year-old, especially one who might beat them soon.

Although I was picking up the pace of my tournaments, mixing in more professional events, I still was going to school as usual. My routine was set: I would go to school from eight in the morning until one-thirty in the afternoon, missing last period because it was physical education (they told me I had enough of that). My mom would take me over to the Kramer Club, where I would take a lesson or practice or wait like everyone else to play an eight-game pro set, because the courts were full. When you waited, you "racked." The process went like this: You put your racquet on a peg, which is tennis's version of taking a number. My friends and I wouldn't sit there and watch other people play, though. We would run to the store to buy candy or run around the block, which featured a treacherous hill. We never sat still. Occasionally, the wait on the weekends was three hours, yet, somehow, by the end of the day, I had played two or three hours of tennis.

My mother always made sure I behaved on court, but I never even considered acting up. I'd only get mad in practice, and even then, it was rare. I did give my racquet a good little tap on the ground every once in a while. I'd tell my mom what all the kids told their parents: "It fell out of my hand while I was serving and it must have cracked."

"We expect her to behave," my mother told Jim Martz, then of *The Miami Herald.* "In practice, after she missed a ball, she kind of took a swing and nicked the court. I'll get on her for that. You can hurt your racquet that way."

I wonder if Mrs. McEnroe ever had that conversation with John.

Actually, I liked to keep my composure, because if I started to act up, I lost my concentration.

And when I came home at nights, I would eat dinner, do homework, and watch TV. I loved TV back then—*Charlie's Angels, Happy Days,* and *Welcome Back Kotter,* especially. At fifteen, I still wasn't dating, just going to movies and parties with my girlfriends. I didn't realize it, but I was so single-minded, I probably couldn't date anybody then. It was not until 1981 that I started dating Matt Anger, my first serious boyfriend. There was just no time for boys in my life when tennis was almost everything.

I was moving very quickly then, much faster than I thought when I kept saying I would go to college and turn pro at age eighteen. By the end of 1977, I was ranked fourth in the country and twelfth in the world. I was named rookie of the year by *Tennis* magazine in 1977. They picked John McEnroe as the men's winner.

In early March 1978, I flew to Dallas for the Virginia Slims tournament there. Everyone has a moment in life that they can look back to and say, "That was it. *That* changed everything." And so it was for me in Dallas.

Why? It was the first time I beat Martina. We were playing in Moody Coliseum on a Friday night in the quarterfinals. Martina was the top seed; I was seventh. They had their biggest crowd ever, nearly nine thousand. They were loud and they loved us. Young versus "old," all the drama of a great upset: What more could you ask for?

As I said, I had lost to her three times before, so I didn't have very high hopes when the match began. But I won the first set, 6–3. Martina came back to win the second, 6–2, setting up the decisive third set. I was down, 5–2, but when Martina served for the match, I hit two great passing shots, then hit a crosscourt backhand to win the game and reach 5–3. I won three of the next four games to tie her 6–6, sending it into a nine-point tiebreaker, when you win by getting to five. At that point, the crowd cheered so loudly, Martina put her hands on her ears, so as not to hear it. At the time I didn't feel sorry for her, but I probably should have. There she was, playing at home, and playing against a kid with no pressure. Talk about impossible.

Anyway, Martina made a couple mistakes, hitting balls into the net, and I was holding a 4–2 lead. Triple-match point.

I got a little tentative and lost the next two points to go to 4–4. That was it. One more point, a simultaneous match point, sudden death, winner take all. I was serving. We returned each other's groundstrokes, then I found an opening and pounded a forehand into the corner to Martina's forehand. She reached it but didn't get anything on it and sent it floating to me at the net. I had a simple crosscourt volley and it was over. Martina had had a thirty-seven-match winning streak, but that, too, was finished.

I remember being so excited I jumped up and down a couple of times at the net. I remember the crowd giving me a standing ovation and Martina, with tears in her eyes, warmly contratulating me and tousling my hair. The newspapers called it the biggest upset of the year. Martina said it was the most exciting match she had had in a couple years. It was the most exciting match I had had in, oh, about fifteen years.

After I beat Martina, I won one more match, an up-and-down 1–6, 6–4, 6–1 victory over Anne Smith the day after the big win, which put me in the final. I became the youngest woman to reach the final since the open era of professional tennis began in 1968. Chris had held that distinction at age fifteen years nine months at a tournament in Charlotte, North Carolina, in 1970. I was fifteen years three months in Dallas.

In the final, I faced Evonne Goolagong, who beat me, 4–6, 6–0, 6–2. There were so many upsets in the tournament that Evonne, then twenty-seven and the mother of a ten-month-old baby, was the only professional left in the semis: Anne, Pam Shriver, and I, teenagers all, were the other three.

When I was growing up, Evonne was my favorite player. I had her autograph my hand when I was a ball girl at the Virginia Slims Championships in Los Angeles—and didn't wash it for days. Evonne and Chris played in the final, with Evonne winning in three sets. Some of the other kids and I waited outside the locker room for about an hour, hoping to talk to them or get an autograph. Finally, Chris came out. I was thrilled. But, right then, Jimmy Connors, her boyfriend at the time, met her and they breezed by us, went up an escalator and—boom—they were gone. Just like a cloud of smoke. I imagine she was pretty upset about losing.

When Evonne came out, she moved slowly down the hallway, signing for everyone. I didn't have a piece of paper (I usually wasn't that unprepared) so she signed my hand.

I told a reporter in 1978 that I most admired Evonne because she was "so feminine and nice and everything." I'll try to be a little more reflective now: She always has amazed me by never seeming nervous. When we met in the semis at Wimbledon in 1980, we both were milling around the seeded players' locker room. It's not a big place, so you each know the other is there. Television sets were turned to the BBC with the matches going on at the time. A British woman who played Wightman Cup took a liking to me and started speaking with me. She talked about my upcoming match—and made me nervous. Arthur Ashe said on TV he thought I was going to win the tournament. That made me more nervous.

And there was Evonne, walking around the locker room, singing a song. She never seemed to have a nerve in her body. She also seemed to enjoy playing very much. I loved to watch her play because she was so fluid, so smooth. It was as if she were out playing in a public park somewhere. She also was a little flighty on the court. She would be hitting groundstrokes almost exclusively, and all of a sudden, she would switch to playing a serve-and-volley game. She would be wailing away, then would begin putting spin on the ball.

After that tournament, I was whipped. I wasn't used to the rigors of the circuit and kept getting more tired every day. I wanted to go home and do some training. I kept thinking, I have to get stronger, I have to get stronger.

At about that time, I began an extensive training program at Laurie Belger's house. It was a secret weight room; secret in that the door was disguised as a part of a wall with pool sticks attached to it. I didn't tell anybody I was working out because it was embarrassing for women to lift weights and sweat. It was a manly thing to do, not feminine. Nowadays, it's the opposite. People sit around the health club for an hour, pick up a five-pound weight for a minute, and claim they worked out.

I lifted on Mondays, Wednesdays, and Fridays and I ran sprints on Tuesdays and Thursdays. It helped my tennis a lot because I started to put on some muscle and add inches to my arms and legs. It also allowed me to stand up to the big girls on the circuit; it gave me confidence.

However, within the next two months, I lost to Virginia Wade and Chris again, but beat Rosie Casals in straight sets. I defaulted in the *Seventeen* magazine twenty-one-and-under tournament in Mission Viejo, California, in May, not long before leaving for England. I had blisters on my feet and couldn't continue.

Why the default? A parent of one of the players started a rumor that I defaulted because I was afraid to play Andrea Jaeger in the next round of the tournament. Andrea was twelve at the time and playing very well. Well, if I was so afraid of her, or the pressure of playing in the juniors, I would have turned pro. I wasn't ducking her: I was hurting.

The rumor led some reporters to ask some of the girls and some of the parents if it was possible I didn't have blisters and simply pulled out because I was afraid of playing Andrea. Some thought I didn't want to have to face her, which was not true at all. Sure, she was younger, but I always played girls my age and under in the age-group tournaments, and almost always beat them. Nothing was different here. I would have played her and beaten her, but I couldn't because of the blisters. To make matters worse, a doctor mistakenly cut away calluses that had developed on my feet, leaving me with the equivalent of third-degree burns. I couldn't play for several days.

I always have hated the way players and parents gossip about other players, and the way reporters pick up on it and blow it out of proportion. I'm one of the first to defend reporters; they have a job to do and most of them do it very well. Some of my good friends are journalists. As I get more and more into commenting, I find myself on that side of the microphone, and I respect and like the job they do. But, fanning the flames, trying to make something out of nothing—that's not acceptable. There I was, all of fifteen and still nearly a year and a half away from my first Open victory, and reporters and parents were making up stories about me. But I found out this happens among the pros as well. When I left tennis, Billie Jean King was quoted as saying I was "burned out" and "afraid to play."

Chris Evert, in her book *Lloyd on Lloyd,* said about me, "Injury and being burned out have since chequered her career." (The book was published in England, which explains the spelling.) What that statement shows is that no one is free from gossip. Everyone takes a shot at you. People don't need facts to make statements. I never burned out, and I certainly wasn't afraid, as Billie Jean had said.

At my second Wimbledon, I was older and wiser and one other thing—sans braces. The tabloids documented my orthodontic work well. I posed with a big smile for several minutes for their "before" and "after" pictures. What a feeling! I was always so embarrassed having them on, especially at fifteen and in high school.

My braces were taken off on May 4. I had told no one I was going to do it. I wanted to walk into school one day and smile at my friends and surprise everyone. But the surprise was on me when the press went bonkers over the fact that I no longer wore braces. As a reporter named Dave Hirshey wrote in a Sunday magazine story: ". . . the world treats your orthodontist's reports like communiqués from the Kremlin."

I went into Wimbledon seeded ninth and came out with more experience and more confidence. Now expected to do well, I reached the round of sixteen before facing Number Two seed and eventual champion Martina for the first time since I beat her in Dallas. She whipped me, 6–2, 6–3. She was too powerful for me, especially with her huge serve—the left-handed slice into my two-handed backhand—and her great deep volleys. I was not strong enough yet to really attack her. Revenge was sweet for her, I know. As disappointed as I was at losing, I told myself to stand in Martina's shoes. She had come back from a devastating loss to me and won big at a more important time. Good for her.

My father told Barry Lorge, then with *The Washington Post,* that he believed I still thought of myself as a little girl. "I think that is why she is so reluctant to turn pro, and we respect that," he said. "When and if she wants to start accepting prize money, we will approve, but at the moment her self-perception is that she is a high school sophomore and not a professional athlete."

My father is a very smart man. He also said in that same interview that he and my mother worried about how I would take it if I ever stopped being as successful as I had been. "I'm surprised at how graciously she loses," he told Barry. "There are usually some private tears for about 10 minutes, and then she's back to normal."

OK, maybe fifteen minutes.

My brother John, who by then was twenty-one and had just turned pro, played mixed doubles with me at Wimbledon, and I also played in the junior girls tournament and won that, beating Hana Mandlikova in the final, 6–0, 3–6, 6–4.

That summer I also learned all about Wimbledon's storied rules. Two hours before my first-round match with Diane Desfor of Long Beach, Robert Lansdorp, my mother, and I were locked out of the All England Club. We got to the large iron gates five minutes before they opened at noon and no matter what we said, the guard would not let us in. The crowd waiting to get in pressed around me, asking for autographs, and I thought I was going to suffocate. I couldn't believe that was the way they treated players. Robert asked if I could just stand inside the fence, and the man still said no. This must have been a big moment in his life because years later, when I was at Wimbledon for NBC, a man came up to me and asked if I remembered him. He told me he was the guard who kept me out. He thought that was pretty funny.

Meanwhile the tabloids were getting meaner and meaner. *The Sun,* Britain's largest-circulation newspaper with four million in daily sales, was reporting an interview I supposedly did with *Women's Own Magazine,* another British publication. In it, I was supposed to have said that some of the other girls—they said I used the word "bitches"—didn't smile or speak to me. They took bits and pieces of interviews I had given the previous year, made up some other quotes, and put it together as if I had written a first-person story. My father was furious and I remember asking the reporters if I was on trial. The tabloids have such power over there.

But I was getting used to this kind of thing, unfortunately. Two books already had been written about me and I had no connection with either of them. One had baby pictures of me I had never seen before. The other book listed someone named Kim Austin in the acknowledgments. There was no such person in my family. In another development, American magazines were calling me Tracy Awesome. Now that one, I liked.

I moved on, making my debut as an Anaheim Orange of World Team Tennis with a win over Wendy Turnbull and playing age-group tournaments the rest of the summer, beating Pam Shriver three times in a row, all in the finals: the 16 nationals, the 18 nationals, and the 18 doubles. I finished third at Mahwah, the event leading to the Open. At the Open, I was seeded fifth and easily reached the quarters, then ran into Chris again. And she sent me packing, 7–5, 6–1.

I remember everyone making a big deal that I had grown to five feet three, which is what the media guide said, but it wasn't quite true. I'd go up to Wendy in the locker room and stand heel-to-heel to measure myself against her because she was about five feet three. And I wasn't.

This was the first Open at the new National Tennis Center, and one that will be remembered as Pam Shriver's entry into the big-time. At sixteen, she was five months older than I was, and there I sat, watching from the stands as Pam upset Martina in the semis to become the youngest women's finalist in Open history. She was six feet, but she had played in my shadow as long as we knew each other. This was the first time she had lasted longer than I had in a tournament. By then, Pam and I already were friendly rivals whose relationship was about to chill, but I must admit that instead of being jealous, I thought her performance took a lot of pressure off me.

In October, I ran my first charity tennis tournament, the Tracy Austin Pro-Celebrity Invitational benefiting the South Bay Children's Health Center. Usually an athlete's charity work begins with the suggestion of an outsider, a gentle nudge, a call for help. So it was with me. Bodie Fite is a wonderful gentleman who, when I was eleven or twelve, practiced with me in the afternoons. He and I used to count how many times we hit the ball back and forth. Sometimes, we would get up to five hundred. By then, we were hitting really softly to keep the rally going.

Bodie was affiliated with the health center, and when California underwent its celebrated budget cuts, very little money was left for the children there. Bodie asked me one day if I would put my name on a tournament to help out. I said yes. He told me more. The money, he said, would go to the health center and its school for children with learning disabilities. The center gave out medical, psychiatric, and dental care either free or at a minimal charge. I thought it was a great idea.

At the beginning, I wasn't as involved as I am now, because I didn't have as much time. So Bodie and Frank Masi, president of the health center, ran the event. I called some friends and asked everyone to help get celebrities to play. Over the years, we've had Dick and Vince Van Patten, Bruce Jenner, Chad Everett, Ron Ely, Robert Duvall, Farrah Fawcett, Kenny

Rogers, Chuck Norris, and John Lloyd, among others. The event is held every year and now is at the West End Tennis and Racquet Club in Torrance, California, where I have played off and on since Robert Lansdorp became the pro there in 1978.

I've always believed in doing charity work, and the older I get, the more I feel that way. It's always great to feel that you give something back to the sport or the people who've helped you. I know I've been blessed with so much. I feel very lucky. I always feel better about myself when I get involved in helping others, whether it's a tennis clinic for inner-city kids in Tennessee, visiting an orphanage in the old East Germany, or seeing the children at the health center.

As an aside, the trip to what then was East Germany was an incredible experience. I went to the orphanage with Mrs. Graf, Steffi's mother, who was terrific. I loved helping the kids, and they seemed so eager to learn the game. I was there in late September and left October 1, 1990, right before the reunification of East and West Germany. We were in several cities, including Berlin. It's been said a thousand times before, but the Eastern part of the city was so sterile, drab, and quiet, while the Western side was bustling with traffic, with much activity going on.

I take particular pride in my own charity, the South Bay Children's Health Center. Over the years, we've raised eight hundred thousand dollars. Without that money, the center would have closed down.

I'm also involved in several other special charities in southern California. Special Olympics is one I love. I go to their state games and help out where I can. I feel like I get more back from those children than I give to them. They are so happy participating in their sports, it brings tears to my eyes.

Then there's Make a Wish, the organization that gives dying children a chance to live out a last wish. I've played tennis with a couple of the children and met others, including a little girl whose arm had been amputated due to something called stone disease, in which the body calcifies. It's very hard to remain cheerful when you think about what they're going through. It's so tough because you get attached to the kids and then you lose them.

I still receive countless requests from other charities for items that can be auctioned—perhaps twenty calls or letters a month. My mom takes care of every one. I give away racquets, hats, and shoes. It takes some time, but my mom and I think it's great, so we do it.

Four days after the charity tournament, two months away from turning sixteen, I turned professional. I really didn't want to. Dick Zausner, a longtime family friend who runs a tennis academy at Port Washington, New York, sat me down in his kitchen after I lost to Chris at the Open and suggested I do it. I've known Dick and his wife, Madeline, since I was eleven and always stayed with them at the Open. I trusted his opinion completely.

I had won the national 16s and 18s and just about everything else that summer. Dick told me there was nothing more for me to do as an amateur. If he had not spoken to me about it, I probably would have waited another year. I loved playing the juniors and loved seeing my game improve against players about my age. I knew if I turned pro, there was no turning back. It was such a strange attitude, but it was the way I felt.

Everyone points to the money. Tennis officials figured out I would have earned $51,687 in prize money to that point that year. I really didn't care. I had no idea how much I would have earned. I wasn't preoccupied with money. On the other hand, as Dick Zausner said, it was time to stop giving it away.

While I was dragged into the professional ranks by friends, kids nowadays turn pro at fourteen or fifteen without giving it a second thought. And, the irony is, it's because they have a precedent: me. It's not wrong, it's just different. I had no one to look to as a benchmark. They now do.

At a press conference, my first agent, Donald Dell of ProServ, was by my side and Sara Kleppinger Forniciari was there, too. So was Bill Ryan, my school counselor, illustrating the two very different sides of my life. Sara and I have laughed about how concerned I was about turning pro. "You had to be convinced nothing in your life was going to change," Sara tells me.

Well, a lot did. The sponsorships and endorsements came almost immediately. Again, I wasn't sure this was something I really wanted. Knudsen Dairy made me their spokesperson, which was great, because we loved the milk and ice cream they brought to the house each Monday. But before the deal started, Sara had to go to Superior Court in Los Angeles to receive approval for the contract because I was a minor.

Other contracts soon followed. Avon hired me as a worldwide spokeswoman for a necklace line called Rising Star, featuring a necklace with three stars on it. I also had a cosmetic line with Avon called Tracy. Canon cameras signed me up, and, eventually, so did Spalding racquets. Overseas, the Gunze clothing company in Japan contracted me to a big endorsement package.

I had to sit for photo-shoots, do commercials, and was interviewed on two-hour-long conference calls, but it was worth it for the money I made. I didn't care then, but it amazes me now. I don't want to get into specific figures, but it's safe to say the endorsements were worth well over two million dollars at that point.

Off I went to Stuttgart, West Germany, with my mother, for my first professional event, the thirty-five-thousand-dollar Colgate series tournament there. It's a unique event because it's played at a small club with one indoor court that seats about three thousand people. It's a homey place where the members take you in and feed you and sell tickets and everything.

I beat Betty Stove in the final, 6–3, 6–3, for the big first-place check of six thousand dollars, and I won the doubles with

Betty as well. Monica and Steffi would laugh at that today. They make that much taking off their warm-ups. If you lose in the first round of the U.S. Open—if you don't even win one point—you get five thousand dollars. But I also had the choice to take a fire-engine-red Porsche 924 worth twenty-four thousand dollars, and I took it rather than the check. What a gift for a fifteen-year-old! I gave it to my mother—what was I going to do with it?—and she drove it until the fall of 1991, when it finally stopped running. She got so attached to the car she hated to give it up.

My mom used to let me practice working the Porsche's stick shift as she took me back and forth to practice, but I didn't like it, and gave up. Then Jeff took me around in the car to practice one day and I got stuck on a hill. A car came up behind me and I got nervous, so I lurched into gear and pulled into a driveway to get out of the way. The car followed me—it was the driver's house. Talk about embarrassing!

Since I needed practice driving, Laurie lent me a green Camaro for a while. When I learned to drive, I bought myself a yellow Mustang. In my career, I was to win four Porsches, two BMWs, a Toyota Supra, and a few others I can't remember. Of all of them, I loved the BMW I won at Eastbourne and drove that one.

Becoming a pro meant two things: I was about to get rich, and I was playing more women's tournaments. I played the Wightman Cup in London and we lost to Great Britain, 4–3—a big upset. They had put both Pam Shriver and me on the team and we just weren't ready for that kind of pressure—the crowd was madly rooting against us and we fell apart. I played Number Two singles and lost my two matches and won in doubles with Billie Jean. Pam was Number Three and lost her only singles match and the doubles as well. Not a good week of tennis.

However, the trappings were wonderful. Attire for the fans was black tie: a crowd in tuxedos. We played in Royal Albert Hall, an ornate, beautiful place across the street from

Hyde Park. Champagne corks popped all the time (talk about distractions). It also was fun for me to play on a team with Chris and the others. We practiced together that week, then prepared to go out and beat each other the next at another tournament. That's the strange and intriguing part of putting athletes from an individual sport together on a team.

My Japanese sponsor Gunze, a company that still produces a Tracy Austin line of women's tennis wear, wanted me to play in a November tournament in Japan, but I didn't particularly want to. It was just too far from home and I was tired from the travel grind. They kept offering me more and more money for an appearance fee—well over a hundred thousand dollars—but I said no. Finally, they offered to fly my whole family over. That did it. We went, and I won easily over Martina in the final, 6–1, 6–1.

The Gunze tournament was held over Thanksgiving. Everyone in my family went sightseeing for the day, but I didn't go because it was too tiring to tour around when I was playing. So Sara and I went to McDonald's for Thanksgiving dinner. People think it's so exciting to travel the world, and it is. But you rarely see cities as a tourist. For a tennis player, it's airports to hotels to arenas.

I played Federation Cup—like Davis Cup for the men, except teams from thirty-two countries play a complete tournament in one week—in Melbourne with Billie Jean, Chris, and Rosie. During the opening ceremonies, when all thirty-two teams marched in with their flags, we noticed a new Soviet player.

"It's Nikita Khrushchev," Chris said.

"Who's she?" I asked.

When everyone stopped laughing, they told me who he was.

"Hey, I haven't taken Russian history yet. I'm only fifteen," I said.

I finished the year with another win over Martina at an exhibition in Long Beach called the Pepsi Challenge; it seemed

I was playing Martina or Chris in every tournament.

The new year of 1979 began with the Rose Bowl parade. I stood on the Avon float and, after about two hours, I had a fun idea of picking roses off the float and tossing them to the crowd. I thought it was humorous; the parade officials weren't so sure. Later that afternoon, I flew to Washington. The tennis year was about to begin again.

I won my third pro tournament in three tries by beating Martina in Washington. I then lost to her five times in a row before defaulting to her in the semis at Eastbourne with an injured groin muscle. The match before the semis, I was playing Ilana Kloss. It had been "spitting," as they call drizzle in Great Britain. The grass was a little damp and she hit wide to my backhand and then, as I ran to get back in position, she wrong-footed me, hitting to my backhand again. I twisted to run toward the ball and slipped and did the splits, pulling a groin muscle.

Eastbourne was a mixed blessing in my career. It's been good to me—I won it a couple times—and bad to me—I've gotten injured there a couple times, too. And the place is odd. The Brits look at it as a seaside resort, yet it's always cold and rainy there in June. But it's a tournament I liked to play because I needed to get used to the surface for Wimbledon. Grass is so different: It's uneven, with terrible, low bounces. Serve-and-volley players have a great advantage on grass. I needed all the practice I could get.

Injuries! When I lost to Martina in the semis in Los Angeles in February 1979, it was the first time I really had trouble with my back. Right before the match, Connie Spooner, the WTA (Women's Tennis Association) trainer, was stretching me—the same resistance exercises we did before each match—and I felt something pop in my back. I could barely get off the table. "What's the deal here?" I said. My back had felt fine, and then it was killing me.

I went out and lost, 6–2, 6–3, and just didn't feel right.

It went away in two days, but in the next couple years, it was going to get much, much worse.

I went from tournament to tournament until I reached the Federation Cup in Madrid in May. I was on the U.S. team with Billie Jean, Rosie, and Chris, who had just gotten married to John Lloyd. That was such a big deal in tennis. I had no idea at the time, but Chris was wondering about her game and looking at me as her top rival.

In her book *Lloyd on Lloyd,* she said when she practiced with me at Federation Cup, she "realized just how hungry and how capable" I was of "taking points and games" off her. The book, written in third-person narrative, says this "served as a warning to Chris of how much Tracy had improved and the growing threat she posed."

The next week, we went to the Italian Open in Rome. It's played on red clay, which makes matches slow and long. Not that Chris and I required that surface for our big semifinal match, since we were so alike and likely to play long matches anyway. But this one was to be especially lengthy—about three and a half hours. Chris came into the Italian having won 125 matches in a row on clay. It was one of her biggest feats—that she had not lost in six years. It was a monumental streak, although, at the time, I don't remember that much being made of it. I certainly didn't think about it then.

I won the first set, 6–4, she won the second, 6–2, and we went to a tiebreaker in the third. How close is that?

On the red clay, you couldn't put the ball away and since we played the same baseline game, points went on for what seemed like hours. They even used different balls, European balls, which were slightly heavier. With the clay hanging on them, they traveled through the air slower. We had red clay all over our shoes, socks, and ankles. It was hot and sticky and we were in for a long afternoon where patience would be as important as any backhand or forehand.

I remember being absolutely exhausted at the beginning of the third set. All I wanted to do was sit down and drink water. Or just sit down—that was my main goal. We were just dying. The balls were getting heavier and bigger. The balls would bounce and grab and you couldn't put anything away. Every great shot I hit, Chris got to, and vice versa.

I was down 2–4 in the third, and I was dead tired. I didn't want to stand up. But I was thinking about my brother Jeff. He would be so proud of me if I just pulled through, I told myself. When he was in law school, he'd meet me at the West End Club and practice with me for an hour and a half in the evening, after I had eaten dinner and done my homework. He would run me hard. I had worked so intensely with him, I didn't want to give up all that tough work, so I pushed all the tiredness out. Just thinking about how happy Jeff would be if I won carried me on.

And I did win, 7–6 in the third, 7–4 in the tiebreaker, on a flailing volley that somehow caught the line, a lucky shot. It was the first time Chris ever had lost 7–6. She said later she was shaky and uncertain and I played with "no nerves." Most of my matches with her were so mental. They were grueling physically, but they were mental most of all. It was who could outlast whom. It also probably was fitting that I ended the streak because I was most like her and clay suited my game just fine, although I hadn't grown up playing on it.

*Lloyd on Lloyd* described the grueling match from Chris's point of view, as told by the book's narrator:

> Chris was devastated by her defeat to Tracy Austin in the semifinals. Tracy, in pigtails, braces and pinafore dresses, was one of the crop of ambitious teenagers Chris' own example as a young prodigy had inspired. What galled Chris was that Tracy was a carbon-copy of herself, but younger and better. She rated her as the Jimmy Connors of women's tennis.
>
> "I knew that unless I was hungry, Tracy would be hard to beat, because she did everything better than me. I was known for my groundstrokes and along came this

little girl who had better groundstrokes. It was the first time someone matched me. She moved better, she hit the ball harder and it was frustrating to have someone eight years younger doing all that to me. She was so young that she could only improve," Chris was quoted as saying.

She also said I won the tiebreaker because I was "more aggressive and took more chances."

The next day, I beat Sylvia Hanika in three sets to win the Italian Open championship, my first major international victory. I don't really remember that match. What comes to mind is how damn sore I was when I woke up that morning. It's not like you get up and you're raring to go. You're stiff and you're tired and everything hurts. You go out to practice and you don't think your feet will ever move again. Those first few balls you hit, you're creaking. It sounds like such a cliché, but you play with pain. You play with bad backs and muscle strains, but you do it because you know you have just one more match to play.

I went home to finish my sophomore year at Rolling Hills High School and had to study nonstop to catch up. By the time I went to England, I was ranked second on the money list, having won $189,500 to Martina's $320,250. The funny thing is, my father still had me on a one-dollar-a-week allowance. Even funnier, the dollar was still important to me. I also got one dollar for every A I received in school. I think my parents kept this up because they wanted me to still have normal, childhood goals.

That summer of 1979 was full of happy memories, not all related to tennis. Cari and I went to the West End Club and watched *General Hospital* every day at two o'clock. That was the summer of the Luke and Laura wedding and I made sure to schedule my practices around the TV show. Some things were more important than tennis. (Well, not really.) I would hit with Mike Flanders, Cari's boyfriend, for three hours. To tell the truth, we hit for an hour and a half and talked for another hour and a half. At night, we had parties at friends' homes, went to movies, went to a Donna Summer concert. I worked hard and I played hard.

After defaulting at Eastbourne, I lost to Martina in the semis at Wimbledon, 7–5, 6–1, which followed beating Billie Jean in the quarters. At my very next event, in San Diego, I beat Martina in the final, then lost to Chris in three sets in the final at Mahwah, leading up to the 1979 Open.

By then, my career had really taken off. And yet, I felt as if I were holding on to a hot-air balloon with weights strapped to my ankles. And I wanted those weights there. My money went right into trust accounts and I rarely spent any of it. We all seemed to ignore it because we didn't want our lives to change. My dad kept his job, of course, but my mom did quit hers at the pro shop when I was fifteen because she was traveling so much with me. I paid her a salary; being with me was hard work. My parents made a lot of sacrifices.

I didn't save every cent I made. I did splurge around Christmas and birthdays. I bought my mom a Rolex watch on one occasion and a full-length mink on another.

As far as my endorsements went, I could have been doing so much more—I had no deals yet on racquets or shoes—but it would have taken up my free time doing commercials for those things, too. So much was happening so fast, I wanted to slow it down. For instance, I was choosing tournaments selectively and never was gone more than three weeks in a row. I didn't want tennis to become a continual grind. I still wanted it to be fun.

Could tennis be enjoyable and still be a job? Absolutely. Most people don't figure out what they want to be when they grow up until they're eighteen, at the very least. At eight, I decided that I wanted to be the best tennis player in the world. From then on, it always was in the back of my mind. I had short-term goals like going to the national 12s, but I always had my dreams, too. I achieved them less than ten years later—while I was still seventeen.

But to meet my goals, I couldn't let up when I was playing tennis. I couldn't be a kid on the court during matches. (Practice was another story.) I learned how to be tough from Robert, my coach. When he came to the United States from Holland, he had no intention of ever becoming a tennis pro. He was a reserve on Holland's 1959 Davis Cup team and came here to get an education when he realized colleges awarded scholarships to tennis players. He went to Pepperdine to become a banker. He did that for a year, hated it, and then got into teaching and coaching tennis.

"Don't ever try to be a nice guy and give them a game," he always said. "If you can beat them love-and-love, then beat them love-and-love."

I was taking Robert at his word.

"You have to go out there and be tough from the beginning," he would tell me. "You can't expect to have an easy match. Get out there and get it over with as quickly as you can."

I know that some wonder why a pro can't let up, can't give up a point in an exhibition, can't be nice. Let me offer an explanation: Every ball I hit in a match had a purpose; everything I did on court, I did for a reason. No false moves. Everything thought out, calculated, planned. Don't get me wrong: I had a great time at practice. I wasn't a machine. I couldn't be intense every minute when I drilled. But it's also true that you can't let up because you don't know how, at least when you're a young pro, on top of the world.

I never had trouble concentrating. I'd develop mental imagery on my own. Nobody told me about it; as my mother would drive me to a match, I just started thinking about what court I would be on; what playing style someone had; if the other player tried something different, what that would be—all the options. Nothing would be sprung on me.

I would actually picture points before a match. I'd hit a

backhand and hit it down the line, and my opponent might hit it crosscourt. I would imagine this the whole time. I would tell myself, "Get the racquet back early, get your feet prepared, step in, make sure your body weight is going forward, lean in, hit it right down the line, then get ready because the other player might get it back." In my mind, I might come to the net and hit a volley. I would say, "I'm going to punch that volley, and I'm going to hit it right in the corner, and I'm going to watch that ball." It sounds rather elementary, but that is the essence of sports psychology. I'd tell myself:

"Do I want to hit it deeper?"

"It's 3–2, it's her serve, I want to break serve here, that'd be great to go up 4–2."

"I'm going to win this point, I'm going to win this point."

"Come on, get tough, get tough, hit it deep, you're going to 'guts' it out."

Your mind is working, always working. You're like a human computer. After every point, I would take it all in, figure out what happened and why, and if it wasn't good, figure out how to change it for the next point. And when it's all going great, you get in a total zone. When you play badly, when you can't concentrate and can't get into the game, you aren't in the zone. That's the term in tennis: the *zone*. You are so focused, you know what the score is, what happened on every point, everything.

In the zone, the ball seems bigger than normal, the crowd is still, everything seems quiet and peaceful, it seems like you're playing in a tunnel. It's a very strange feeling but a wonderful one, because you feel so powerful, you can hit the ball as hard as you want, everything's going in, you're moving effortlessly that day. Those are the matches you live for. They are few and far between, but they are worth it. You move and you run and it's easy. You're really relaxed, even on the tight points.

Two perfect examples are two matches I played within

three weeks of each other against Ivanna Madruga of Argentina in April 1980. The first was in the semis at Hilton Head, where I beat her in three sets, 6–3 in the third, in three hours. It was a struggle. She was impossible to put away on clay.

Three weeks later, we met again on hard courts in the quarterfinals of the Tournament of Champions in Orlando. I beat her, 6–0, 6–0, in thirty-nine minutes. She won eleven points. That day, everything seemed brighter and easier for me. I felt so effortless being out there. The change in surfaces made a difference, but not that much of one. I just was in the zone.

I had had glimmers of that feeling at other times in my career. I was in the zone throughout many of my junior days. I certainly had the feeling against Martina when I beat her in Dallas in 1978. But I wasn't going to know the feeling for good until a few sunny September days in 1979.

# Chapter Four

$S$unday, September 9, 1979, was a sunny, pleasant, late summer day in New York City. I began the day by hitting some balls on the backyard court of our friends the Zausners. I ended the day standing in line in my tennis dress at McDonald's. In between, I won the U.S. Open.

We had a one-hour drive to the National Tennis Center in Flushing, New York, from the Zausners' home in Sands Point, New York. In all my Open matches, I never warmed up at the tennis center. I always hit with Robert, my coach, at the Zausners' for forty-five minutes: crosscourt shots, down the line, volleys, overheads, and serves. Everyone has a different warm-up routine: from what I've noticed, Monica Seles always plays points. Martina and Chris do a variety of things: rallying and playing out points. Steffi rallies with her coach and goes for the corners.

One thing about the circuit is that with all the indoor tournaments, a lot of times there is just one court in an arena, so four of you are out there, hitting crosscourts, down-the-lines, whatever.

That morning, I practiced my forty-five minutes, then my mother, father, Jeff, and I got in the car for the drive to my match with Chris Evert for the prestigious Open championship, which Chris had won four times in a row. It was my first Grand Slam final. As my dad drove, Jeff got me started on tongue twisters and kept me giggling. He had flown in from Los Angeles the day before just to see me play in the final. This, of course, meant everything to me.

I wasn't nervous as we neared the National Tennis Center; I was unbelievably relaxed. I guess I was oblivious to what was about to happen to me. Most times before matches, I grew quite quiet, but not this time. I was a live wire, but it wasn't nerves. It was just being sixteen, I think, and not realizing the magnitude of the event.

I also was very prepared. I had a routine: I liked to be in the locker room at least an hour before I played to shower, get dressed, get taped (my feet were the main problem, with those blisters), stretch, do my hair, and put on makeup. Yes, makeup I didn't wear a lot but I always put some on. One thing you learn really fast is to use just a little mascara—and the waterproof kind. When you perspire, it can get awfully messy around your eyes.

Some players come in ten minutes before they play and just take a shower, get dressed, and go out and play. They don't take any quiet time, which is fine for them, but that never worked for me. I liked to have a lot of calm time. I didn't like to feel rushed before I played.

Choosing the dress before the match was easy for me. I was superstitious. I wore a pink dress, which is what I always wore against Chris. I always wore a peach dress when I played Martina. Chris put on her favorite dress at the time, which was a white dress with some pink satin trim at the top. It seemed like she always wore that for the final.

Two guards escorted us from the nearly empty locker room to the Stadium Court. Right before we went out onto the court, Chris and I were jockeying for position for what might sound like a silly reason. I wanted to sit on the bench to the umpire's left. I had sat on the left all week and felt superstitious about it. I sensed that Chris wanted the left side, too, so we both tried to get in place by hugging the wall across from that bench. I got there first and stayed put, so when we emerged on the court, all I had to do was walk across it and put my things down on the bench to the left. Chris had to walk on the other side and got the right bench.

As Chris (the top seed) and I (the third seed) walked out to hit for a few minutes before our match, I noticed my family and coach were already in place. My mother and Robert were in the Zausners' box at one end of the stadium; my father and Jeff were sitting together at the other end in the players' family box.

I don't put that many demands on my family, but I absolutely had to know where they were sitting and told them not to move during the match. I wanted my parents to be in one spot, especially my mother, who was there with me almost all the time. She had her superstitions, too. For example, she always lined up her bracelets on her wrist in a certain way when I was playing.

My rule for my parents and family went for boyfriends and surrogate parents, too. At Wimbledon a few years later, Matt Anger, my boyfriend at the time, was reading the paper as I was warming up. "This is the quarterfinals and he's reading the paper!" I said to myself. "This is not Sunday morning in L.A." I looked over and motioned for him to put away the paper. I was so nervous, I wanted him to be nervous, too. I wanted him to watch every minute.

And I'll always remember Ellie Appling of Memphis, in whose home I stayed when I was playing junior tennis. She became "my mother for the week" during one tournament and didn't move from her seat during even one of my points. I thought she was going to have a nervous breakdown by the end, but she loved every minute of it. I still see her every year when she and her husband come out to Los Angeles on business.

I must have driven everyone nuts at one time or another. Earlier at this Open, my father settled into his seat near the end where I was warming up before a match and pulled out his camera and telephoto lens. I walked over to him. "Please put the camera away, Dad," I said.

My father said OK. I walked back and hit a few more balls. I looked back to see the camera was still in his hands but the telephoto lens was off. He thought that was what was bothering me.

I walked back over. "Please, Dad, I mean the camera," I said.

My father put it down, by his feet. I noticed that, too, and went back to him again. "In the case, please."

In the case it went. My father understood. I was worried about the match and when I looked over at him, I wanted to see his face, not a camera. But this created a very funny situation that now is represented in a photo hanging on the wall at my parents' home. The very moment I won the 1979 Open, a photographer took a picture of me that shows, in the background, my father and Jeff in their seats. In the picture, Jeff is leaping to his feet. But my father is leaning down, reaching for something on the ground: his heretofore hidden camera.

We still laugh about the picture to this day.

The shadows were long and the lights were on when Chris and I began playing late in the afternoon. We played pretty evenly through the first four games, then Chris broke my serve to go up, 3–2.

The first game, I tried to get out all my nervousness, especially from my legs. I wanted to find the range of the court and try to set a strategy. I felt myself hitting the ball deep, hard, and consistently; everything felt good. I felt in command of the court.

At 2–3, I broke Chris, then she broke me, and I broke her again, so we were at 4–4. I won my serve and then took the first set, 6–4, when Chris hit a forehand long at 30–40 on her serve. Breaking serve wasn't as big a deal in our matches as it was against Martina because neither of us had monstrous serves.

I had no unusual or surprising strategy going into the match. I told myself just to hit the ball deep and keep her moving, which is exactly what I did on the last point of the first set. I ran her from a deep backhand to a deep forehand, which she lunged for and hit out.

If there was one thing you wanted to do against Chris, it was to hit deep. She had a lethal drop shot, especially from her forehand side, which she disguised very well. It looked like she was going to hit a regular slice and at the last second, she would hit a drop shot. I also knew I needed to take balls out of the air if I could and put them away. I wanted to end the points a little sooner and be more aggressive. I didn't want to just rally at the baseline, even though that happened a lot.

I breezed through the first three games of the second set to jump to a commanding 3–0 lead. Winning that first game was so important; my mother had always said that the first game of the second set was the chance to keep it going if you were ahead or change things if you were behind. It's a vital psychological game, and I won it at the net, of all places, where Chris brought me with a drop shot.

At 3–0, I remember the crowd becoming very quiet. I don't think the fans knew what to do. I mean, Chris was losing. What a shocker.

Chris reacted by hitting the ball harder. She went for more winners when she was behind, took more risks. Overall, I hit the ball harder than she did, but she was trying anything. Statisticians figured out we were hitting the ball an average of twenty-five times a point. She certainly wasn't giving up.

Meanwhile, my mind started wandering. I began to think about what would happen if I won. I wasn't concentrating, which was really stupid because two weeks earlier, I was leading 4–2 in the second set against Chris at Mahwah, then lost that set, 6–4, and the third set, 6–1, when, once again, I was bothered by blisters. Now, I was doing it again. I wasn't playing in the present. I started playing carefully, instead of playing the way that had gotten me to that point. I had to force myself to keep driving the ball and not just play it safe. Not coincidentally, Chris fought back to 3–2, then I broke her for 4–2 and won my serve to go up 5–2. Chris held for 5–3 before I won it all on my serve.

In the final game, I fell behind love–30, then 15–40, giving Chris two break points. But Chris netted a forehand return on one serve to go to 30–40 and I hit a backhand winner up the line for deuce. That was one of my favorite shots. I always felt confident with it and tried to use it as a surprise after a few backhand crosscourts. After Chris hit a forehand long for my advantage, she weakly hit my second serve into the net and that was it, 6–3.

I jumped into the air, ran to the net, and warmly shook Chris's hand. She patted me on the head. I looked back toward my dad and Jeff. It's funny when I watch the tape of the match (which is hardly ever), I realize CBS never, ever showed my mother, father, or Jeff. Maybe they didn't know where they were. Or who they were.

When I watch the tape, I realize how powerful-less our match looks. There doesn't appear to be much power or pace. The irony is we hit the ball very hard, but it doesn't look like it because we played with wood racquets, which are obsolete now, of course. I get miffed sometimes when people say we don't look powerful, because the game has changed so much. That was the way the game was played then, and we were the best out there that day. Today, with a composition racquet, my serve is much more powerful, and so are my groundstrokes. But the seemingly radical changes didn't occur only with the women's game. When I go back and watch the John McEnroe–Björn Borg "match of the century" from Wimbledon, they look powerful-less, too.

And so, I won. It's funny; I don't remember much of

what happened next. There is so much to take in and it all happens so fast. Everyone runs onto the court so quickly, they interview you and give you the trophy (it was so heavy that I rested it on top of my head), and in fifteen minutes, it's all over. They shepherd you to the press room, where all the reporters ask all their questions. I don't remember any of those, but I do recall that Laurie Belger—"Some Man"—handed me an ice cream cone. A just dessert, perhaps?

On the court, Tim Ryan of CBS interviewed me briefly. I still laugh when I listen to my answer to the question of why I played so well.

"A friend of mine is into astrology and she said yesterday and today were my best days," I said.

Tim asked if I believed in astrology.

"No, but my friend does."

What a ridiculous answer. Oh well, I was sixteen.

Even more crazy is the fact that I received hundreds of letters from people who were into astrology, most asking my sign. We had someone answer them all, saying I wasn't into it after all. I had to nip that one in the bud.

Minutes after the match ended, Chris bumped into my father under the stands. They had never met before. "Congratulations, Mr. Austin," Chris said. "Your daughter played very well. I'm very happy for you."

I will never forget that Chris did that. It was such a classy move.

Now that I had become the youngest women's U.S. Open champion (at least for now, because Jennifer Capriati has a shot at it in 1992), I grabbed my stuff and, still in my pink tennis dress, left the Tennis Center and jumped back into the car with my mother to take my father and Jeff to JFK Airport. My dad had to go to work on Monday morning and Jeff had to get back to law school. It's crazy to think we didn't hire a car to take them, but it was such a great moment, we all wanted to be together. We all laughed and smiled and were as happy as could be. It was a very warm feeling. I immediately knew what I had done, which was win the U.S. Open, and I was thrilled. However, I didn't realize then it was that big a deal, that it would be mentioned every time I was introduced from then on.

My mother and I dropped them off and then, on our way back to the Zausners', we got totally lost. I was getting hungry, so my mom pulled into a McDonald's. Now wearing a sweater over my tennis dress, I walked in and got in line.

A lot of people stared.

"I just saw you on TV," one guy said. "What are you doing at McDonald's?"

"I'm hungry," I said.

I ordered the usual—quarter-pounder, Coke, and fries—and left with my mom.

Junk-food pit stops were nothing new for me. At the 1977 Open, my brother John and I stopped at Baskin-Robbins daily for a pint of mint chocolate chip ice cream after our matches. The difference between this one and that one was now I was the U.S. Open champion, and no one expected me to be celebrating my victory at McDonald's.

By the way, all this discussion of junk food requires a defense of my eating habits now. I wouldn't eat any of that stuff today. I eat much healthier food now. Honest.

The morning after my victory, *Good Morning America* wanted me on their show, and they did a very smart thing, considering how lost my mom and I got the night before. They sent a limo for us. Then we went to a pet store and I bought the Zausners a gift, a little black Pekingese. The dog they had before was a brown Pekingese named Georgia. He was my favorite dog and, when he died, I wanted to give the Zausners a new one. For the first hour, the dog just sat there. He wouldn't move. I thought there was something wrong with him. But he got better and the Zausners named him Wilson—for the racquet I used to win the Open. I switched racquets the next year, but as far as I know, there are no dogs named Spalding running around Long Island.

Bringing up Wilson reminds me that when I won the Open, I was not paid by Wilson to use that racquet. I had zillions of Wilson racquets given to me, but I didn't have a contract with the company. That is absolutely unheard of now, and they are huge, huge deals. Clothing is the same way, but again, I not only wasn't being paid to wear a certain line of clothes at that time, I was paying Ted Tinling for my dresses. I found a receipt not long ago: eight hundred dollars for eight dresses made especially for Wimbledon. They had to be predominantly white; Martina once wore a navy-blue collar and thin navy-blue stripes on her dress, and Wimbledon officials measured it to make sure the majority of the outfit was white.

I was resisting endorsements even after the Open. They wanted me to endorse a Tracy Austin doll. I said no. It seemed silly to me. Now I think maybe I should have done more of that, but I didn't want to be bothered. I also have to say, somewhat mischievously, at sixteen, you want to try to feel grown-up and I didn't want to be associated with dolls. I did a 7Up commercial once and the reason I did it was it took only one day to shoot. My agent back then recently told me that I made four times what John McEnroe made to do the same commercial. I got a hundred thousand dollars.

The point is that I wouldn't have had a life had I done everything that was being asked of me. Winning the Open was worth hundreds of thousands of dollars—millions, perhaps—not just the thirty-nine-thousand-dollar check I received. But enough was enough. Every day was so precious. I had to have a life.

I think about that all the time. Not long ago, I noticed that Jennifer Capriati was one of many people on the cover of the *Guinness Book of World Records,* and she probably doesn't even know about it. Or care. Most people never will have their photo in the newspaper, much less on the cover of a book. We tennis players and other professional athletes have it so good, we sometimes don't even realize it. We're so busy we don't have time to think about it.

The 1979 U.S. Open was more than the final against Chris. Getting there, I played six matches and five of them were two sets. Only my fourth-round match against Kathy Jordan went three sets, and, while I don't like to offer excuses, one of the reasons why I had trouble was I got my period that day. I always lost my coordination the first day, and that was what happened out on the court but I still won, 4–6, 6–1, 7–6. Some women get terrible cramps; I just lost my coordination. It's something every female athlete deals with, although no one ever talks about it in public. You never hear it brought up at a press conference. I don't know why that is, really; I guess it's simply too personal.

Not that what happened to me against Kathy was that bad. Top seeds like to have a scare in the early rounds of a big tournament to wake up. It's like a blast of cold water in the morning. Against Kathy, in the third set, I had to fight off six break points, trailed 5–6, and had a match point against me before winning. All of a sudden, I was looser. Nothing seemed so bad after having a scare like that.

And nothing was. I steamrolled past Sylvia Hanika, 6–1, 6–1, then eked by Martina in the semis, 7–5, 7–5. By then, I was five feet four and a hundred-fifteen pounds, so I was better able to compete with Martina. The *Los Angeles Times* called me "a backboard in sneakers." I played a solid match with good service returns and good passing shots. The lob was also effective in keeping Martina off the net.

"Finally, I'm in the final of something big!" I exclaimed in the interview room.

Right after my win over Martina, I called Jeff, who had promised to fly out if I made it to the final. Interestingly, my match was to be shown on television on a tape-delayed basis on the West Coast, but Jeff must have forgotten about the time change.

"You better come," I said to him on the phone.

"Don't be so cocky," he said. "You haven't won yet."

"Yes, I have. You're forgetting the time difference. It's already happened."

I went back to school on Tuesday for my junior year at Rolling Hills High. A banner read, CONGRATULATIONS TRACY—OUR CHAMP. I hated the attention—really. It embarrassed me. I wanted to be average and blend in. Also, I really was shy about my success. At my request, the school kicked out photographers and reporters. I had classes to take and didn't want my tennis to intrude on my other life. I was on the cover of *Sports Illustrated* and was proud of it, but I also sensed my friends at the club were jealous. I didn't want to make a big deal out of anything.

The rest of the year was a mixed bag: semifinal losses to Wendy and Evonne (twice) in Avon events; a big win over Martina in the final at Stuttgart in November, and my second Porsche (could it be just a year since I turned pro there?); and another over Martina for a hundred-thousand-dollar first prize in an exhibition featuring the top four women in the world in Japan. I finished the year ranked third behind Martina and Chris and also was named Associated Press female athlete of the year. My sister accepted the award for me down in Florida because I was in school, plus all the appearances and travel became too much. As I look back on it now, I did miss out on a lot of things that, were they happening today, I would cherish. Now approaching age thirty, I definitely would go to receive that award in person.

The eighties soon began—and for me, professionally, they didn't last very long. Going into the decade, everyone said I was headed for superstardom, Wimbledon victories, more U.S. Open titles, and who was I not to believe?

Especially the way the decade started. The Colgate series finals were in Washington just after New Year's, and there, I beat Chris twice in three days. It was a double-elimination event to the semis. I beat Chris, 6–1, 6–3, then, 6–3, 6–0. (I lost to Martina in the final just as badly, 6–2, 6–1.) Then, a week later, in the final in Cincinnati, I beat Chris again, 6–2, 6–1. I felt so confident playing her, I was dictating play. That was three times in eleven days. It just about rocked her out of the game. She appeared on the cover of *People* with her husband, John Lloyd, saying she was quitting. As she later wrote in her book, it bothered her that I was this young person coming up behind her and beating her. Then she decided to come back and had some pretty good tennis left in her, but, hey, it was a good story for a while.

After I beat her in Cincinnati, I walked into the locker room and looked through a big glass window to see Chris crying in the training room. It really shook me up to see her crying so hard. She was used to winning tournaments; she had been queen for so long. I was younger and I was American, just like she was, and that made it worse. I could feel she was in a lot of pain. So, all of a sudden, my happiness over winning was gone. I was looking at a person who was crumbling and I felt so bad. I got out of there as fast as I could.

Even though I had been on the circuit for a couple years, I still felt like an outsider with some of the women. There was a clique that included people like Rosie Casals, Chris, Martina, and Connie Spooner, our trainer, and I definitely was not a part of it. I was too young and perhaps too good. I was an outsider and they would not let me in. I knew when I played one of them, the others would be rooting against me. That didn't feel too good, but it made me want to win even more.

I started to make my own friends: Bettina Bunge, Jeanne Duvall, and Anna Maria Fernandez. I had people my own age to hang around with and feel more comfortable with. I still mostly stayed to myself, however. My mother and/or my agent Sara would travel with me to every tournament and would either share my hotel room or stay in a nearby room. My social life consisted of room service so I could do my homework. Sara still teases me about the time I ordered a steak at the Omni Hotel in Atlanta and, when it came sitting in half an inch of grease I patted it dry with a hotel towel. I led a relatively dull existence on the circuit, but I believed my tennis required it. I had to stay focused on one thing, and tennis was it. It sometimes wasn't easy keeping up with my homework because I had to play Martina or Chris the next day, so I wasn't really concerned about studying geometry. But Robert or Sara would help me if I got stuck on something. Math always was the toughest because if you get behind, you're dead. I remember endless nights of Dad trying to explain formulas at 1:00 A.M. My mom and Sara, meanwhile, became great tourists and pals, visiting everything from Versailles and the Berlin Wall to the hotel bar.

I was not too interested in sightseeing. After I won the Italian Open at age sixteen, for instance, my mom and I raced through the Vatican in twenty minutes—then dashed to the airport.

As far as tennis went, things just kept getting better for me personally. I went over one million in earnings at age seventeen. It happened at the Wells Fargo tournament and the people running the event didn't miss their chance to make the most of it. They held a press conference and two armed guards accompanied a truck filled with one million dollars—in bags—into the arena. I laughed, but I couldn't keep it.

Much more important, though, I became the Number One woman player in the world on April 8, 1980. I found out when my mother whispered it into my ear.

I had been on quite a roll—winning the Avon Championships in New York, then the Clairol Crown at La Costa, both over Martina. After beating Renée Richards at Hilton Head in the Family Circle Cup, I was sitting at the table in the interview room, waiting for the reporters to file in, when my mom came up to me and said the rankings were out and I was Number One. I couldn't believe it, it was hard to imagine, almost intangible. It was something I'd always wanted. I had become Number One on this whole earth.

But if I'll always fondly remember 1980 as being the year

in which I was ranked Number One, I'll also remember it sadly as the year I should have won the Wimbledon singles title.

I won my two tournaments prior to Wimbledon—the Federation Cup in West Berlin and the Wimbledon prep at Eastbourne. At Wimbledon, I had some trouble with Barbara Potter in the third round—it took three sets—but otherwise had straight-set victories heading into my semifinal match with Evonne Goolagong.

Barbara was one of the women I most respected on the circuit. She worked so hard and showed so much determination without having the most talent. At Wimbledon, she was very difficult to beat because her left-handed serve was impossible to return. The serve was Barbara's forte. She would practice it an hour a day and, by sheer will, she made it a huge weapon. At Wimbledon, there was some mud where I stood to return serve and I got stuck in it throughout our match, slipping to try to return her serve. She had the perfect game for grass: great serve, good volleys, and slices so the ball stayed low.

More important, she is a really good person. Barbara was very nice to me through my injuries, sending me books, keeping in touch, and checking to see how I was doing. Barbara definitely was one of the smartest people on the tour; I've heard she's going to college now, which takes a lot of initiative for a woman our age. Knowing Barbara, I'm sure she's working harder than all her fellow students.

In the semis, I lost to Evonne, 6–3 in the first set, then beat her 6–0. But I blew it in the third, losing 6–4, and also losing my best chance ever to win Wimbledon.

If there's one match in my whole career I could change, it would be that one. If I could have beaten Evonne, I would have played Chris, who by then had returned to the game. I had beaten her five times in a row, scores like 6–1 and 6–2. I had just killed her.

That was running through my mind as I entered the final

set with Evonne. And, right at that moment, I lost the match. I let up; I stopped playing as aggressively; I stopped making my deep shots; I was no longer dictating points. I was in a fog.

Evonne was such an unpredictable player; the toughest to play from that standpoint. You never knew what she would throw at you. Against me, she started to come to the net. She was so difficult to play on grass because she hit a lot of chop shots that just died there. That was what she was doing to me. Soon, the match was over. I wanted so much to win—and lost because of it. It's strange how you sometimes never get the things you want the most.

But there was a silver lining in the clouds over Great Britain that summer. I always dreamed of winning Wimbledon and I did, in a way. My brother John and I won the mixed doubles.

We had played together the year before and it was such a terrible experience, I didn't want to play mixed doubles again. We met Marty Riessen, my future coach, and Wendy Turnbull in the first round and Marty was all over the net—poaching, slamming balls at me, and hitting the ball so hard, I was miserable. After we lost, I told John, "I'm not doing this anymore. I'm uncomfortable out here."

John convinced me to try again in 1980. It had been a rainy week, so we began play in the first round on the second Thursday of competition and ended Sunday, four days later. The day after I lost to Evonne, I had to play her again—with her Australian partner, John Newcombe. When my brother John saw the draw, and saw we were playing Goolagong and Newcombe, the Number Three seeds, he booked a flight home. No one gave us much of a chance. But we played them anyway, and, down a set, we beat them, 6–4 in the third. The highlight for me was acing John Newcombe on my second serve when we were down in the third set. He was receiving on the backhand side and cheated into the alley to be able to use his forehand on my second serve. Well, I put it right down the middle and he didn't have a chance. He just about died.

He hated being aced by a woman—and on a second serve, no less. Whenever I see him, I still tease him about it.

In the quarters, we faced Virginia Wade and Vijay Amritraj. We fell behind, 4–1, in the third set, and it was my serve. That was not good. I was nervous.

"Whatever happens, don't panic," John told me on the changeover.

I won my serve and we came back and won the match. John went out and had two T-shirts made: WHATEVER HAPPENS, DON'T PANIC, the shirts read.

Each victory elevated us to a new emotional high. We pulled out one, then another, then another. It was so much fun to be doing this with my brother, with our family there to watch us. Each night at dinner, we'd say, "How did we do that?"

We went to the final and beat Mark Edmondson and Dianne Fromholtz, 4–6, 7–6, 6–3, to win the Wimbledon mixed doubles championship. It was a gray day, but I was beaming as my brother hugged me on Centre Court. On the BBC broadcast, the announcer said something that still rings in my ears: "This is a young lady who I'm quite sure is destined to appear many, many more times in Wimbledon finals on this very court."

Unfortunately, he was wrong. There would be only one more, a second-place finish in the mixed doubles the next year.

Injuries—the signature of the rest of my career—were about to take hold of me. In Mahwah, New Jersey, leading up to the 1980 Open, I lost to Andrea Jaeger in three sets in the quarters because I was not in shape due to injuries. I had trouble with pulled hamstrings that summer after Wimbledon and never felt good. I pulled one hamstring and when I came back, I pulled the other hamstring: dueling hamstrings.

Because of these problems, I spent more time than usual at the beach that summer—and less time on the court. I had begun dating my first high-school boyfriend, Tony Rickard, a friend of Cari's. Tony drove a pickup truck and we would go out to dinner and go to parties with friends—the usual things kids did before their senior year of high school. Except, for me, it was very unusual because I should have been playing tennis and instead, was living a normal life.

I played just two tournaments between Wimbledon and the U.S. Open, where, as defending champion, I lost to Chris in three sets in the semis. I won the first set, 6–4, then lost, 6–1, 6–1. I expended all my energy in the first set and was totally pooped the rest of the way. It was a huge match for her, having come back from that little retirement. She went on to win her fifth title in six years and I went home, knowing I had to stretch more and get in better shape, especially for more endurance in the third set.

I played sparingly that fall. In the final of the Tampa tournament, I was in such pain I had to default to Andrea. You don't default finals, but I had to. My leg and my rear were hurting me, right where they connect. It hurt when I hit a shot and even more when I rotated into a shot. I went to some doctors. They told me I had a pulled muscle and to get more therapy and rest. The result of rest: Your body goes to pot.

I started undergoing therapy that just wasn't working. No one knew what it was. I tried to touch my toes and I was so stiff, I couldn't do any better than three inches above my ankles. I had always been stiff; my friend Anna Maria and I used to wear sweatpants when we warmed up during our Friday workouts with Robert so he couldn't see we were bending our knees as we touched our toes. If he caught us, we had to run laps around the court. He rarely noticed. That was funny. This was not. At that point, no one even knew about sciatica, which is what I ended up having, an inflammation of the sciatic nerve that runs from the lower back down the back of the thighs. Doctors said I either had a problem with the top of my hamstring or the lower part of my rear end. No one knew what was wrong with me.

I played three more tournaments through January 1981. The last was the Colgate Championships of Washington. A bad snowstorm outside pushed the indoor event back a day, allowing me to spend the off-day in treatment with Dr. Steve Haas, an orthopedic surgeon, before playing the final against Andrea. I didn't practice the day before, I was just visiting doctors. Somehow, I won, 6–2, 6–2, probably because I was in such pain, I had to concentrate more.

But that victory was deceiving. I was in trouble.

From January until May, I left the circuit. After going nuts at home in California, I decided, together with my mother, that I needed a change of scenery. Luckily, it worked. I flew to New York to stay with Dick and Madeline Zausner and play on the indoor courts at the Port Washington Tennis Academy. Although it was winter, I wanted to be around a tennis atmosphere. I always had fun at the academy, plus things had changed at the Kramer Club. I was eighteen now and Anna Maria, Anna Lucia, and Trey all were going to USC. I didn't have many people to play with at home. I needed a fresh perspective, and Dick, who was the one who convinced me to turn pro, always was there for me. They took me in like a daughter.

The first week I was there, I was confined to my bed with a corset on. I looked out my window and watched snowflakes fall. It was so cold and white outside. All I did was stay in bed, read, and do my homework, which I sent back to school so I could finish my senior year. I had a light load the last semester. I was depressed and quite lonely. Is this what my career had come to, injured and huddled under the covers at age eighteen? Only one year ago, I was Number One. Now I was stuck in bed and very scared.

Fortunately, things got better, slowly but surely. When the pain started to ease, I stretched a little and took short walks. Then I began to do more. Dr. Irving Glick, who played at Port Washington, came by every day and put me through strengthening exercises. I was scrawny, I had lost all my muscle tone, and it required weeks to get it back. Dick took me out on the courts one day. The first day, I played seven minutes. The next day, I played fourteen minutes, until the pain got too bad and I stopped. I built it up from there, playing each day until I couldn't move, it hurt so badly.

I began playing with Bob Binns, the head pro at the academy. He was very patient with me and helped me build on each day. Eventually, I was playing two to two and a half hours a day. The pain was not 100 percent gone, but I felt ready enough to come back to competitive tennis.

Anxious beyond belief, I returned in May for the Gunze tournament in Tokyo. I reached the final, where Andrea beat me in the third set in a tiebreaker. I was just glad to be playing again. I finally had built myself up to where I thought I could play again, but I found out that even though my sciatic nerve problem was fine, I was extremely sore from playing again. It doesn't matter how long you practice; when you start to play tournaments, your muscles get more tense from the nerves and competition so you end up extra sore. I felt sick and sad as I went to the airport. And lonely. I wanted someone to talk to, to share my problems with. For the first time ever, I began to think about dating someone seriously.

I had broken up with Tony when I went to Port Washington and went out on a few dates when I was there. I enjoyed having someone in my life, even if he was a friend. But with all my travel and my injuries, I knew I wanted something—and someone—more than that. I wanted a life full of more than just tennis.

But first, more tennis. I flew directly from Tokyo to West Berlin, going from an indoor rubberized surface to outdoor clay on a different continent. In Tokyo, I went straight from that three-set match to the airport and a fourteen-hour flight to Germany. Talk about stiffening up. Japan Airlines actually had beds on its planes—"I'll have a nonsmoking bed, please"—but it still was a grueling schedule.

When I got to West Berlin, I couldn't practice for the first two days. I could barely lift my legs. My hip flexors, the muscles that allow you to lift your legs, were so sore I could not walk. I lost in the quarters, went home for a while, calmed down, practiced, and got in better shape. The tournaments went on without me. I decided to set my sights for Wimbledon.

The good news was I won Eastbourne very easily, defeating Andrea in the final. I was thrilled with my performance, having beaten Anne Smith, a great serve-and-volley, grass-court player, and Barbara Potter along the way. I played six matches and after every one, I went back to the hotel and sat on two bags of ice, one for each cheek.

Now for the bad news: I seemed ready for Wimbledon, but I lost to Pam Shriver in straight sets in the quarters, 7–5, 6–4. It was the first time I had lost to her. But it wasn't all bad news at Wimbledon: I started dating Matt Anger, who won the junior Wimbledon title and became my first serious boyfriend. I came home and went to the Wightman Cup in Chicago and won two matches, but, mostly, I remember practicing like a banshee. I was furious with myself because what once was my forte—concentration—now was my weakness. I had not gotten it back completely since my four-month winter layoff. I had real trouble staying focused in a match. Concentration is like a muscle: If you don't use it, you'll lose it. I realized I had become very negative about my game and I hated that I was like that, but I couldn't stop it.

I would say things to myself during a match: "You're making too many errors. Why are you making so many mistakes? Where has your concentration gone?" These thoughts don't help in any way. All you're doing is pronouncing the negative.

To get out of this, I had to rebuild my mental game from the ground up. I told myself to ignore the big picture and focus on the small things: hitting the ball deep, moving my feet, those kinds of things. I had to force myself to think positively about my game. It's no different for the player at the local club; forget the negative, go back to the basics.

In August, I moved onto the Canadian Open, which probably was my best tournament ever, although no one paid much attention to it, then or now. I beat Pam in the quarters, Martina in the semis, and Chris in the final. I obviously had my concentration and confidence back.

But that also was the tournament where I was reduced to tears when Pam Shriver called me "a fucking asshole" as we shook hands after the match.

That explosion requires some explanation. I beat Pam nine times in a row in age-group competition and kept on beating her in the pros. I had lost to her at Wimbledon but came right back to beat her at the Wells Fargo tournament in Rancho Bernardo, California. She was very critical of me, which I guess I can understand, because I was doing better and receiving more endorsement contracts and was just better known. Basically, I bugged her. Once she called me "that little twerp." I guess I was little compared to her six feet one inch.

Pam says we first met when we were at the twelve-and-under nationals in Savannah, although I don't remember her. She was playing "Crazy 8s" or some card game and she made a dumb move. I was standing behind her, watching, and, according to her, I said, "That was stupid."

She turned around and glared at me. "Shut up or I'll step on you," she said, according to her book.

I don't remember any of that, either.

I must admit that our relationship didn't get much better over the years we played one another. It didn't help that I always beat her. At the junior girls team intersectionals (Southern California versus Middle Atlantic, and the like) near Philadelphia in 1977, Pam was up a set and leading, 5–2, in the second set, ready to win, when billowy black clouds rolled up.

"Come on rain," I thought to myself. "Come on rain."

Sure enough, it poured. Our match was postponed until the next day, but the grass was so wet, we had to move to hard courts, a much better surface for me. Grass is perfect for a serve-and-volleyer like Pam because the ball comes off the ground low and fast, with an uneven bounce. Hard courts produce a more even, higher bounce.

Pam was upset at the lost opportunity because it gave me a chance to come back. And I did, winning 7–5 in the second set and 6–0 in the third. In other words, eleven consecutive games.

Our relationship dropped to its lowest point in Toronto at the Canadian Open four years later.

Pam was acting like a baby, throwing her racquet, going nuts on the court. The chair umpire overruled seven points in our match, five of them for me. Both numbers were unusually high. Pam actually lay down on the court after one of them. I just stood there, watching her. I never did anything like that and I frankly was surprised she was acting so badly, but she gets pretty emotional on the court.

So, when I won match point for a 6–2, 7–5 victory, I took the ball I had in my front pocket and bounced it behind me as I began walking toward the net. She saw me do that—not exactly an overwhelming emotional display, especially considering what people do today when they win—and laid into me when I reached out to shake her hand.

"You're a fucking asshole," she said as she shook my hand. "You're a bitch."

Whatever happened to "Nice match"?

It sounds stupid now, but I was so shocked by her language, I went over to my seat, sat down, and cried. When the reporters asked me why I was crying after the match, I had to say something. So I said she used some unpleasant language that began with an *F*. Needless to say, that made all the wire services and became big news in Canada, which rankled Pam all the more.

So Pam had a full head of steam when she sat down a few years ago to write her book, *Passing Shots,* which came out in 1987. I can't believe how rude she was to me. In some ways, I hate to bring up all these critical things, but I feel I need to defend myself. So, here goes:

She got into everything. She said I "dumped" ProServ, Donald Dell's management company, when I did not. I simply left when I could after my brother Jeff and a group of agents split from Dell to form Advantage International. She also wrote: "I thought ProServ did a great job marketing Tracy, especially given her personality and her public-speaking ability."

Come on. Sara Kleppinger Forniciari was turning down tons of deals for me.

It gets worse.

She wrote that I won two U.S. Opens "with the worst serve I have ever seen."

Even the photo cutlines weren't safe: "The late, great Tracy Austin. Did you hear the one about Tracy making a comeback? Miss ya, kid."

She got on my mother several times. Once, she mentioned my mother saying her three sons had never been around language like Pam used with me at the net at the Canadian Open.

"Very sheltered family, the Austins," Pam wrote.

Perhaps my mother overstated the case a bit, but most mothers hope their boys don't say those words, and furthermore, Pam was wrong to swear and my mother was right to criticize her.

Pam also laid into my mother about coming into the locker room before matches:

> Mrs. Austin and Tracy would even lock themselves into one of the toilet stalls. I can remember being at tournaments where I'd actually see two pairs of legs under the door! One year at Wimbledon I was scheduled to play Tracy on Centre Court. Now, Centre Court matches go on like clockwork; 2 P.M. precisely means precisely 2 P.M. Well, Tracy was famous for never being able to get out

of the bathroom on time, prematch nerves and all that. Before this one match, Tracy and her mother were in the W.C. for an age! Tracy was never as popular with the girls as she could have been, and I think part of the reason was that we never really got to know her without her mother around.

This other stuff I can tolerate, but criticism of my mother goes way beyond common decency. Again, I feel compelled to defend myself because all this is out there for anyone to read. Yes, my mother did come into the bathroom stall with me once, in the seeded-players' locker room at Wimbledon, but I needed to talk to her about something. The stall was the only place we could be completely alone. There was no other place where we could talk privately. My mother was my best friend on the circuit; no doubt about it. I needed her, and what she provided for me in moral support and advice goes way beyond the strange appearance of four legs under a stall door.

She's right about the bathroom. I always spent the last minute in the bathroom. I still do when I give a speech or do commentary, but I was never late.

I give credit to Pam for being so strong and self-assured as a teenager. I would guess most kids would have real trouble dealing with the pressures of tour life—and the pressures of winning, which I certainly was doing more than Pam—and would need a safe refuge. I was fortunate to have a mother who could and would travel with me. If we sneaked away to a private spot to talk about prematch jitters, so be it.

Pam and I even met at the White House once. At a tournament for Mrs. Reagan's antidrug campaign, Secretary of State George Shultz and Pam were talking, when Mr. Shultz said, "Did you hear Tracy Austin is making a comeback?"

Pam said, "It seems like I've heard that one before."

I was standing right behind her and could hear every word. I couldn't believe she was taking her little problems right into the White House. I wanted to blast her, but I just chirped something rather kind about her needling me. I don't know why I let her off the hook, but I did. I guess I didn't want to have a fight with her in front of the Secretary of State.

Finally, I had had enough. At the U.S. Open after her book came out, I went up to Pam and said we really had to talk. I hadn't been on the circuit in five years or so and I wondered why she kept taking pot shots at me. I mean, what kind of target was I, just sitting there? We had known each other forever and we were the same age, so we had some things in common. Then there were the differences: East Coast/West Coast, tall/short, demonstrative/quiet. So we had lunch at the U.S. Open Club and talked things out. I didn't know then if we'd be better friends or just coexist peacefully, but I knew things couldn't be any worse than they had been.

In February 1989, I ran into Pam again while we both were playing an exhibition in Detroit. Pam's life was so full—with businesses, travel, charities, the works—and she was so confused that she almost had a nervous breakdown. She wanted to hire a secretary. She didn't know what to do about this or that. My sister Pam and I were there, and she just talked incessantly to us, nonstop, she was so confused. And I spent a lot of time listening, because I could identify with her feelings.

She and I met again at Amelia Island, Florida, where we practiced together. Every five minutes, Pam would come to the net and say, "Let's do this business deal," and lay out some idea she had. This was about the time Martina dropped her as a doubles partner because Pam was so mixed up. I know this sounds strange, but I was glad I was there for her. She was going through what I had gone through several years earlier, including injuries and the inevitable ending of her career, so I was glad I could be a sounding board for her.

Because of her injuries and numerous business commitments, Pam hasn't played singles at the top level for several years now. However, she still is a very good doubles player because she is smart, has a huge serve, volleys well, and plays the percentages well. I don't think she's been in great shape lately, and that has affected her as well. But priorities change. I certainly understand that.

Perhaps because of this, things continue to be good between us. Although my mom and Jeff won't ever say Pam's name because they are so angry with her, I really feel if she and I lived closer, we would be very good friends. We have so many common experiences, it would make sense. I think she's hilarious and she thinks I'm not so bad. It's kind of like Chris and me—we are fierce rivals who try to push the tough matches behind us.

Pam and I played doubles together in Zurich in 1988 and got along great. The promoter of the tournament invited us to take a helicopter ride in the Alps region one day. Pam couldn't go because she had a singles match, but I went. He told me we were going to have lunch with "someone special" in Zermatt, by the Matterhorn. I thought it might be Pirmin Zurbriggen, the Swiss skier.

I was wrong. When we landed, we did indeed see a skier waiting for us. When I jumped out, I realized who it was—Chris Evert, on skis. Andy Mill, her new husband, was filming his TV ski show there. We had lunch and then I went back to the tournament.

Throughout that week with Pam Shriver, there was a silent, nagging reminder that she once was very rude to me. All in all, I try to forget. And, apparently, so does Pam. She was one of just a few players who visited me in the hospital after my car accident in August 1989. She definitely understands injuries: She came on television with me on USA Network at the U.S. Open in 1991 with her wrist, elbow, and shoulder wrapped in ice. That's the reward she gets for playing so much tennis.

Back to 1981. After beating Pam at the Canadian, I defeated the usual duo, Martina and Chris, for the title. My hamstrings had calmed down for a while. I was back playing my best tennis of the year. And another U.S. Open was right around the corner.

# CHAPTER FIVE

Martina Navratilova has always been one of the people I admire in tennis. Just as I am, she is much more emotional than she seems. She is one of the smartest people in our game. And she was great fun to play against, because our games were so different and she was so competitive.

It was very fitting that I met Martina in the final of the 1981 U.S. Open, the last Grand Slam singles final of my career. To me, she is the bridge between the women's game of the seventies—the game of Margaret Court and Billie Jean King and the young Chris Evert—and the game of the nineties—the Monicas, Jennifers, Steffis, etc.

She never has been loved as much as Chris by the American sports public, which is a shame, because she is a wonderful person, very sensitive and caring. And she is so incredibly smart and well-read. Whenever I talk to Martina, I end up discussing politics, the arts, or other sports. Not tennis. For instance, it was so characteristic of her to say what she said when Magic Johnson announced he had the HIV virus. She said that a woman athlete would not be treated as a heroine, as Magic was a hero, if she were in the same situation, and she criticized Magic for sending a mixed message about safe sex when promiscuity was one of the problems with AIDS. I know Magic and feel so sad for him. I went to his New Year's Eve party in 1990; he put a tent over his tennis court and met everyone at the gate and just was so genuinely happy to have all his friends around him. I still see him riding the exercise bike when I go for therapy at the Kerlan-Jobe orthopedic clinic. I cried off and on for a week when I heard the news about him. I was moved again when I watched the All-Star Game as his fellow basketball players gave him so much respect and hugged him. He's a great example of someone who handles adversity well.

But I also agree with Martina, that there is a double standard for men and women regarding sexual promiscuity. She deserves more endorsement contracts, but she doesn't get them because she has admitted she is bisexual. A man like Wilt Chamberlain can admit to sleeping with twenty thousand women and people laugh and wink. If I slept with hundreds of men and talked about it, I would have none of the corporate deals I have today. Everything I have—product endorsements, corporate clinics, other appearances, and television assignments—probably would be gone.

I went into the 1981 Open as the third seed (behind Chris and Andrea) and was really fit, the thinnest of my adult life, about one hundred and ten pounds. Perhaps I was too thin, as I look back at it. But I won every match in straight sets leading up to the final. I was healthy and so happy. This was my tournament, I told myself. Martina and I had to wait for the finish of the men's semifinal between John McEnroe and Vitas Gerulaitis, one of those five-set marathon matches. I got dressed and taped and stretched out and was all ready, psyched up just perfectly. And then we had to wait and wait and wait. I was sitting in the players' lounge with my mom and it was like a ghost town. Martina was there, walking around, but everyone else was gone by then. I ate half a bagel. I got nervous. I walked around. I watched the men's match. By the time I got onto the court, my emotions were spent. I was drained from being psyched so long.

And then, in the first set, Martina, who was seeded fourth, just blew me away. I lost that set, 6–1, in twenty-five minutes. A fan told me later that he went to get a Coke, waited in line for a few minutes, and came back to his seat to find out the first set was over.

Martina, obviously, started out like gangbusters. It was embarrassing. I was awful, a nervous wreck. The wind was swirling, playing havoc with our serves, with drop shots, with lobs, you name it. Martina had four service winners in the first game, then won five straight points in the third game after I had her love–40 on her serve. My serve, never a strong point in my game, drifted in the wind. Martina's was strong, whereas mine wasn't. I never focused on it, never thought about it much, and therefore never worried that it wasn't all that effective. I much preferred to work on my service returns and passing shots. But it still looked particularly bad in that first set.

What was I thinking when I lost 6–1 in twenty-five minutes—it felt like ten minutes—on national TV? I was embarrassed beyond belief. I had two choices: fall completely apart and get out of there in another twenty-five minutes, or, try, somehow, to get back into the match. I felt my stomach tighten at the thought of coming back. Two sets? Against Martina? How in the world was I going to turn this thing around?

And then, I thought, I've been doing it for most of the year, with my injuries. Taking slow steps, going day by day. On the tennis court, day by day equates to point by point. I said to myself, "Tracy, you're on national TV; go one point at a time and you're not going to embarrass yourself."

This really is where mind strength came in. I could have just folded at that point. Martina was playing well, I was playing poorly. I wasn't adjusting very well to the conditions. But I started to set short, achievable goals. I didn't want to think of the big outcome because that was overwhelming. "Just one point at a time. One point at a time. Those points will string together.''

And the points did come together. And then the games came together. Soon, the match was mine.

I had some strategic tinkering to do as well. I had to think about what I was doing wrong. For me that day, it was my feet. I wasn't moving them. Most of the time if you don't play well, you are not moving your feet. I needed to keep the ball in play, to extend points, to make Martina play another shot, then another, then another. She was more likely to make mistakes when that happened, and drawing out points was a style more to my liking. I wasn't going to win without gaining control of the match.

I was serving at 4–4 in the second set when Martina had double break point. But she made unforced errors on every point and I held on to win the game. We reached 6–6 and I took the tiebreaker, 7–4. In the third set, we again reached 6–6, but I won the tiebreaker, 7–1. Martina was getting tired. She had played a three-set match the day before against Chris in the semis, and after playing for another two-plus hours against me, she was becoming fatigued. Twice in the tiebreaker, I beat her with forehand winners down the line, past her forehand. That was most unusual. I spent the day hitting to her backhand, which is considered her weaker shot. I changed up and caught her flatfooted. She said later she was tired, and I don't blame her. I was, too, and I had had a much easier semifinal match against Barbara Potter, who won only four games in two sets.

Near the end of our match, Martina started crying. She had never won the Open at that point, and she was so devastated, she began crying before we were finished. On match point, she double-faulted. I don't think she could see through her tears.

The awards ceremony is a blur for me. I don't remember anything, except that Martina couldn't stop crying. I was so unbelievably happy, but I felt terrible. I mean, how can you celebrate when a person you like and respect is crying in front of you? It took away most of my joy, which was a shame. I never had a more fulfilling victory, winning the first U.S. Open women's title ever decided by a tiebreaker. I never had a greater comeback on the court. If anyone doubted my ability as a fighter, I had this victory to show. It was my total victory, one I appreciated so much more than the first Open title in 1979. This one, I had to fight for. After being flat on my back in bed in March, I had not lost between Wimbledon and the Open and then took that title. I came back to play my very best tennis.

That night, I didn't go to McDonald's for my victory dinner. My family, the Zausners, the Belgers, Sara, and I went to dinner in Port Washington. It wasn't a fast-food place. True to another tradition, however, I did receive another ice-cream cone at the press conference.

I was now graduated from high school and wasn't going to college, so I played throughout the fall, with relatively few injuries. College wasn't an option then. I was playing too well to stop my career. I did get to enjoy the college experience with Matt, who went to U.S.C. We were always there with his friends.

I went to my first Australian Open and lost to Pam Shriver in the quarters. The Australian was on grass then, her favorite surface. My passing shots were not quite precise enough to beat her on that day. I had never played the Australian or the French Open before because of school. The Australian takes up two and a half weeks in December by the time you travel over and back; the French takes another two and a half weeks in May. My mother suggested to me that I could get a tutor, but I was adamant about not missing school. It sounds strange, I know, because I could have won both of them, perhaps several times, but that wasn't the point. I was in high school and there was no way I could travel to those places and still have somewhat of a normal school life. I do regret that now; the years I could have won the French and Australian, I didn't play them.

After losing to Pam, I played the Toyota Championships at the Meadowlands. I played Chris in the second round and lost 7–6 in the third in more than three hours. It was a round-robin format where losers played the next day and winners had the day off. So, with every muscle hurting, I mean, just aching, I walked into the locker room the next night and the first thing I saw was Chris getting a massage on the table. Great, I thought, I have to go out and play another match and she's having a massage. If a few more points had gone my way, *I* would have been on the table and *she* would have had to go out to play.

I won that match in three long sets and still have no idea how I dragged myself out of bed the next day to play Chris again, because I was so sore. I beat her in the semis—drilled her 1 and 2—and then took a three-setter from Martina to win the tournament. It was a matter of pushing the tiredness out and perhaps being able to concentrate more because I knew I had just a little energy left. I couldn't last forever, so I had to be more focused on each point. But I was in really good shape to come back and win after such a tough match the day before. Plus, there was the image of Chris on the massage table and me trudging out to play again. Sometimes, you need that kind of motivation.

I was hoping to get the Number One ranking for 1981 and thought my performance at Toyota would seal it. But Chris got it, in spite of the fact that I won the Open, had a great tournament record, and beat her more often than she beat me. I also beat Martina head-to-head that year. I imagine I was penalized for missing several months due to my back problems. My year was shorter than everyone else's.

A few things were happening during that time that added some turbulence to my life. Earlier in 1981, I changed coaches. I moved out of my parents' house and bought my own place in 1982. My back, which was completely fine at the end of 1981, got worse in 1982. And I was going to face more difficult moments as my tennis career again was put in jeopardy that year.

On the coaching front, Robert was suing me. Just your minor little *People's Court* squabble between friends. Actually, it was very traumatic for me and hurt a lot. We had a mutual split in January 1980 and things were tenuous for a couple years, back and forth. He said he was getting tired of my attitude, and I was getting tired of *his* moods and attitude. I think he also was upset that Roy Emerson was helping to coach me. Tennis players often get help from other people every now and then; this was no different. I began working with Roy because he lived close in Newport Beach and because he could help me more with my serve and my net game. Robert is a fabulous teacher of technique and groundstrokes, which is why those were my strengths. I needed help with my serve and volleys, so I went to Roy for that. Robert had a very hard time sharing his pupils with anyone. He is very possessive.

I believe I treated Robert well. I don't think I ever was a brat or anything like that; I was a perfectionist. I remember that Robert flew all night to coach me at Hilton Head in 1980, right after I became Number One and a few months after our breakup. As we warmed up, I became more and more agitated. He couldn't get the ball in.

"Robert, if you can't hit the ball in, consistently, I'm going to get somebody else," I yelled to him. The poor guy, he had just flown in on the red eye and I was all over him. Now, I can't believe I acted that way, but at the time it was natural. I was that intense. Boy, professional athletes can be very demanding. Scott Holt, my boyfriend now, says I'm still that way. When we practice, I expect a 100 percent effort from him and 110 percent from myself. To be Number One, you have to be that way, though. I needed ten hours of sleep, and I usually got it. I had to eat at the right times and needed to have the understanding and support of people around me and basically lived a rather selfish life. This is not unusual. This is typical behavior for all of the top athletes I know. For that matter, any successful person has to be somewhat selfish.

The problem that led to the lawsuit was that Robert wanted a guaranteed amount in coaching fees, while Donald Dell and ProServ said they thought they could get Robert a specified amount in endorsements and contracts of his own because he was my coach. There was confusion about whether the endorsement fees were to be part of the guarantee or in addition to it.

When Robert didn't get the endorsements, he sued, even though he had been paid the guaranteed amount. We settled for a smaller sum out of court.

I got mad at everyone. I thought Donald should have avoided the confusion in the first place and Robert was just plain greedy. I didn't want a coach who was suing me and my management group, so I fired him. I hired Marty Riessen, the former pro, who is a wonderful man, and he helped me through the next Open. Marty is totally different from Robert. He had me work more on strategy and on different strokes. It was exciting to hear new ideas. He would write down a few strategy points before I played and we discussed them. I continued to work out at the West End Club and continued to see Robert, but I didn't practice with him. He kept saying he wanted to work with me again. So, like the scorned wife who keeps going back to her husband, I went back to him. Perhaps I should have dumped him for good, but I was loathe to change. Look at the examples in my life: I waited longer than many would have to turn pro; I wanted to keep going to school; I didn't get a tutor. I just hated change. Then again, Robert, for all this negative publicity, was a great coach and a good person for me—as long as we stayed on the tennis court and out of the courtroom.

I also stayed with ProServ—because of my great relationship with Sara—until my brother left there in 1983 with a group of employees to form Advantage International, also in Washington. There was a clause in the agreement between the two firms that said I couldn't move to the newly formed rival management group for three years, so I left ProServ as soon as I could, jumped to International Management Group out of Cleveland in 1984 for two years, and then went to Jeff at Advantage in 1986. When I was leaving ProServ, Sara flew to Japan to see me to try to get me to stay. I wasn't leaving because of her. She was great. ProServ was trying to keep me under contract, and I felt like I was being held hostage.

At about the same time, I was in the process of moving out of my parents' home. It was time: I would turn twenty at the end of 1982. I no longer was a child. So I made a big break: I bought a two-bedroom condo ten minutes away from home, two doors from my brother John. It was hard leaving my parents, but I wanted to be a little more independent. In spite of myself, I wanted to do things on my own, trust my own judgment. I wanted to become more autonomous because I was at the typical age where I was trying to find my independence and didn't agree with my parents on everything. I needed to break away some from the mother-daughter bond and develop a relationship between two adults.

One of the first people to ask me about moving out was Chris Evert. We were playing in Berlin in 1982 and she heard me talking to some of the other players about buying a condo. I was nineteen, she was twenty-seven. She said to me, "I wish I'd done that. I wished I had lived alone."

Chris moved from her parents' home in Fort Lauderdale to her own house with her first husband, John Lloyd. She was like many athletes, myself included, who had so many things taken care of by other people. When that happens, it's hard to know what you really can do.

Chris later was divorced from John and married former Olympic skier Andy Mill. Wolf Mack, my boyfriend at the time, was with me when I ran into them at George Bush's inauguration in January 1989 in Washington. They asked me when I was going to get married.

"Who knows?" I said. I asked Andy when they would have kids.

"When Chris figures out she can do something else besides play tennis," he said.

We've all seen she has adjusted quite well to motherhood.

Most athletes have to prepare to leave their sport. I understand this because the same thing happened to me. Tennis was my identity and it disappeared when I got injured. I didn't have anything else. I felt naked. I had trouble watching matches on television, as Chris told me she did. There was a huge void. But I started to fill it: I began to do commentary, I started to travel, I dated men seriously, I developed girlfriends who knew nothing about tennis. They weren't always saying, "Great match—Saw your interview. . . ." They would say, "Cute pants you have on." Finally, normal conversations.

What I had before was a tennis identity only. As in: Tracy Austin equals tennis. That's the way it was until the early 1980s. And then, when my career fell apart, I became Tracy, the person. I wasn't averse to working on a TV crew and trying new things. I was excited about the prospect of learning. My identity was not just tennis. I was more than that.

I visited Chris in Florida right after she had her son, Alex, in the fall of 1991. I went to see her baby and give him a present. It was a nice visit and it got me to thinking about our relationship. There had always been a wall of competitiveness stemming from our intense rivalry. I hope as time goes on, we can put that in the past because we have so much in common. It really would be nice to compare notes: how people have reacted to early fame, how it affected family, friends, and the men in our life.

We always have been looked at in the same light by the American public. We appear to be the same, coming from Catholic families and tennis families, hitting two-handed backhands, and leading about as normal a life as possible in this game. I was supposed to be her clone. We even went out with the same guy, TV commentator Bill Macatee, both briefly—and definitely not at the same time.

Chris and I had our differences and she has given me a hard time about them, though usually in a good-natured way. But not always.

At the Federation Cup in Australia, she asked me if I ever smoked pot. I was not yet sixteen. When I said no, I never had, she ripped into me. "You're so sheltered," she said.

At Wimbledon the next summer, Chris, Virginia Ruzici, a couple other players, and I were chatting in the locker room. Actually, they were talking and I was listening. They were discussing the first time they slept with a guy. They never looked at me. I was sixteen. They knew I didn't have an answer yet.

When I was seventeen, Chris told a story one day about getting drunk. She glanced at me. I said I never had gotten drunk. She berated me for that one, too.

Chris always was very aware of her public image. She probably will be voted America's female sports heroine of the century, that's how popular she is. She openly talked about a very public affair with Adam Faith, the British rock star, and even after that, came out smelling like a rose. Overall, the positive aspects of her image—formed during seventeen successful years on the circuit—are so strong that things that might have tarnished it did not.

I held a 9–8 edge over Chris in our matches over the years, and I played her only as a teenager. I never played her after the age of twenty. I wonder what my record might have been against her had I continued playing. She had more trouble with me than any other player at that time.

Robert Lansdorp delighted in my victories over Chris. He used to whistle when I played her and he knew it bugged her, so he did it some more. A few years ago, Melissa Gurney, a young charge of Robert's, was playing Chris at a Manhattan Beach tournament. Melissa was doing very well, so, on a change-over in the third set, Robert whistled his whistle and yelled out to Melissa, "Come on, Tracy!" Chris turned her head, looked up, caught Robert's eye, and glared at him. Robert shrugged. When he told me later, I was embarrassed. If I had been there, I would have told him to stop. Chris came back and won, probably inspired by Robert's antics.

Chris had a lot of responsibility in women's tennis. Because she was and is so popular, she undergoes more scrutiny and criticism than most of the rest of us. Billie Jean King was the pioneer, leading us into the glory days of the eighties and nineties. Without her, we wouldn't be even close to where we are today, and I think the only top player out there now who realizes this is Martina. Chris, meanwhile, was our savior. She couldn't have come along at a better time. When Billie Jean admitted her affair with a female hair dresser, she lost all her corporate contracts and endorsements, but it didn't ruin our sport because we had Chris. Chris is beloved because she was so feminine in an era when many of our top women's sports stars were not. And she was so young: the girl next door. I think that's why people liked me, too.

Chris made millions because of this image and Martina lost millions because of it. It's so unfair, but that's Madison Avenue. Martina has been open about her sexuality and has been hurt because of her honesty. Yet I do think the public has come a long way; I don't look at Martina and think that she's bisexual. I look at someone who's bright and funny. After all the publicity and tears from Judy Nelson, Martina's former lover, at the 1991 Wimbledon, I called Martina on the phone and told her I would be there for her, and if she ever needed to talk to anyone, she could call on me. Martina is a friend of mine who has helped the women's tennis tour tremendously, although she probably has hurt herself in the process by being so honest and not hiding her sexuality.

As for my image, I soon became invisible on the circuit. I was struggling with injuries in 1982 and 1983 and made just two brief appearances in 1984. When an athlete is injured, she must allow time to heal and then recondition and rebuild. The strength, stamina, and endurance that sustained me through the U.S. Open in 1981 vanished. My body kept sending out warning signals of aches, pains, and worse, but my head refused to listen, because it never had had to listen before. My tunnel vision finally was getting the better of me. My mind and body weren't working together anymore. Was I to work harder or take a break? But if I stopped, how would I ever find my mental strength again?

You know that if you ever get too comfortable with normal life, you might not have the same intensity again. I needed to have that edge and not get soft. Once you stop, you start to think too much and lose confidence. So I told myself, "You're fine." But I wasn't fine.

On January 12, 1982, one year to the day after my back became so painful in Washington, I hurt it again. I defaulted in the second round of the Cincinnati tournament and went to another orthopedic surgeon. I tried doctors in Los Angeles and nothing worked, so, finally, I went to a chiropractor, Dr. Leroy Perry. He watched me walk and scanned videos of my matches and noticed that I had overdeveloped the muscles in the back of my legs and on the right side of my back, while my stomach muscles were weak. As a result, my spine was out of place and pinching my sciatic nerve.

He started with simple stomach-strengthening exercises and stretching lightly. He adjusted me and had me hang upside down to stretch out my spine. The pain started to go away, and by April, I was hitting the ball again. But I was in such limbo. It wasn't as though I had a fracture and knew I would be in a cast six and a half weeks and then out. This was uncharted territory. When one bad thing happened, others seemed to follow. Even freak accidents. As I walked to the ladies' room at a restaurant, a waitress bumped into me and spilled scalding water on my left arm, causing second-degree burns.

The Women's Tennis Association wasn't exactly thrilled

that I was out. In fact, WTA officials pushed me to keep on playing, or at least say I was playing. Peachy Kellmeyer, assistant executive director, called me almost every morning, usually at seven o'clock, to ask me or my mom if I was going to play in the next tournament. They needed either Chris, Martina, or me—the top three at the time—in each event. Peachy would tell me to go ahead and enter a tournament and hope to play, and then, if I wanted to pull out, that would be OK. Dumb me, I did it. I would enter, say, Kansas City, then look like a goofball because I'd pull out of Kansas City and have to pay a fine because I withdrew late. The newspapers would get angry and everyone would hate me for not coming to their city when I wasn't planning on being there anyway. It was hard to explain I was injured, because then they'd ask why I entered in the first place.

If I were doing this now, I would never have been pushed around by the WTA the way I was then. It was crazy. In fact, because of Andrea Jaeger and me having so many injuries so young, they now know better than to put pressure on kids coming up.

Why was I not well? One reason was God didn't give me a body that was 5 feet 9 inches and 135 pounds. I was tiny and susceptible to injury. Just think of the blisters: They were a hindrance, but I played on. I have unusual feet, narrower than average at the back and wider than usual by my toes. I always had blisters on the balls of my feet and on my little toes. My coach, Marty Riessen, would cut a tiny X in my nice new shoes by my little toe just to give me some room.

Also, off-court training didn't play as big a role then as it does today. I'm stronger and I think in better shape at age twenty-nine than I was at nineteen. Now, I work with a trainer, Ken Matsuda, who lives ten minutes from my house. If only I had known he was so close ten years ago. My back and ligaments and tendons can take the punishment today. My back hasn't hurt in years because of the daily stretching and strengthening I do on all the equipment in Ken's basement. Ken started me slowly, beginning with exercises with big rubber bands and cords, as well as exercise in the pool. The secret to my success with Ken was that he started me slowly and helped me build a firm foundation, something I needed all along. Swimming, for example, is a good workout with no impact on the body. The only thing that hurts today is my right knee, the one with the screw below it from my accident. It will never be the same. I am reminded of that every time I work out.

No one really was into training the way players are now. Look at the circuit: Martina never reached her full potential until Nancy Lieberman got her going in 1981; Chris was not in great shape until the early 1980s. No one trained with weights or ran. We worked hard on the court but not off the court. Because I was smaller than the others, I was more susceptible to physical problems.

I went to Wimbledon in 1982 and lost to Billie Jean in three sets in the quarters: 3–6, 6–4, 6–2. It was the first time I ever lost to her. I wasn't feeling prepared and I didn't have much confidence. I used to know I could hit a certain shot because I hit it twenty times in practice the day before. Now, I wasn't able to practice much, so I didn't walk out onto the court knowing I was going to win.

I lost to Hana Mandlikova in the quarters, 4–6, 6–4, 6–4, at the Open that year, my first loss to her. I won the first set and was up, 4–1, in the second when it started to rain. We had to finish the next day and it was cold and I couldn't get warmed up. But that's no excuse. Hana came out firing and was too tough to beat.

I won only one tournament in 1982, in San Diego. I had won twelve in 1980 and seven in 1981. But I still finished the year ranked fourth, which meant that I was not playing all that badly. I played consistently through the year. I simply wasn't winning as many events.

My problems continued in 1983. I made the semifinals in

Houston and Chicago and reached the final at Hilton Head before losing to Martina in three sets.

I pointed toward Wimbledon. But in my zeal to get ready for Wimbledon, I overtrained at Eastbourne, the warm-up tournament, and had to default in the semifinals. I was training with Tony Roche, the Australian player and coach. I went to Eastbourne a week early and worked with him two hours in the morning and two more in the afternoon, which was like playing eight hours a day with somebody else. Tony is that tough on you. So tough, in fact, that I ended up with a stress fracture in my back.

I didn't know how serious it was at first. I knew my back was sore, so I took a steamy shower before I played each match to try to loosen up. But my back ached so badly that I could barely turn on my backhand. It got worse with each match. I finally had to default in the semis to Wendy Turnbull.

I went to Wimbledon seeded fourth, hoping that I might get better. I didn't and had to default there, too.

I had been playing so well after hitting with Tony that I was really looking forward to Wimbledon. I tried to give my back as much time as possible to heal, so I didn't do anything except rest and receive ultrasound for a few days.

But in the morning of my first-round match, I went out to warm up and knew when I tried my first backhand that there was no way I could play. It was so disappointing to be there—one hour away from starting Wimbledon—and to be injured again.

I went back to California, had X rays in Long Beach, and was out six weeks. I barely remember what I did. My boyfriend of several years, Matt Anger, was gone quite a bit, playing tennis. I traveled to Washington to watch him play and stayed at Sara's house. I did very little else. I was bored. Then, the very first day I was allowed to practice, I was so preoccupied with getting ready for the U.S. Open, I played for three hours, got tendinitis in my shoulder and missed the Open and the rest of the year. How dumb could I be? People who stay at the top stay prepared. That was a prime example of not being prepared. I wasn't even myself. I was being silly. I heard a Chinese proverb once: With time and patience, the mulberry leaf becomes silk. I didn't take the time or have the patience to heal. My body was screaming, "Slow down!" But my mind still wasn't listening.

My mother thinks at that point, my tremendous drive is what did me in. I tried so hard because that was all I knew. I know it sounds incredibly stupid now, but I didn't know any better, and no one advised me otherwise. All I knew was hard work on the tennis court. This time, instead of helping me, it hurt me.

In September, I flew to Australia to work with Tony. Talk about being "down under." I was supposed to go there and come back healthy and ready to go. I stayed until December 12, my twenty-first birthday, in the hope that this would be the miracle cure. Everyone thought I needed intensive training to beat the injuries. This was a classic case of letting others run my life. I didn't know what to do and didn't trust my own instincts, so I thought I would try it. My agent and friends thought it would be a good idea to do something radical, to move to Australia for three months, to see if I could come back stronger and free of injuries.

Tony was the perfect guy to go to because he works his players very hard; it's that Australian work ethic personified by Tony, Roy Emerson, and Ken Rosewall, among others. They all grew up with Harry Hopman, who drilled them to death.

With great results. I admire the Australians. I've hit with Ken Rosewall and he hits the ball so heavily. What I mean by that is he hits behind the ball with topspin, so when it hits your racquet, it feels like a ton of bricks. The impact shoots up your arm.

In Australia, I got up every day, ran two miles, practiced two hours, ate lunch, practiced another two hours, lifted weights, ran sprints on Tony's backyard tennis court, had one hour of deep massage, and went to bed in a little room at the Roches'.

It was a dreadful routine. I was sore, lonely, and hating it all at once. I thought it was good for me at the time, because I always knew hard work is what worked for me. I really liked working with Tony, but now I know it was too much. Nobody can lift weights with the same parts of the body every day.

To make matters worse, this was the first time I had been away from home for so long. My family and friends weren't there, and I especially missed Matt. He and I talked every day on the phone. It didn't help much. I still was thousands of miles away from him.

I had no car and was stuck in this place called Turramurra, an hour outside Sydney. I was too worn out to go anywhere anyway. I also wasn't particularly interested in venturing out in a country where people drive on the other side of the road. This was miserable. This was hell. Yet I wanted to play so badly I would try anything.

I paid Tony twenty-five thousand dollars for this experience. It sounds like I spent a lot of money until you consider that I then played three exhibitions—in Seoul, Jakarta, and Hong Kong—that earned me a total of seventy-five thousand dollars.

In spite of those engagements, this was when I began to let go of tennis. The sport was deserting me; I wasn't deserting it. I came away from the three months with terrible shoulder tendinitis. I had tried everything except letting my body heal with time. I was being forced to start to live a life, a real life, beyond center court.

Why, I asked myself, was I putting this kind of pressure on myself? Then again, what's left if I can't be Number One? I'm a tennis player. What else do I really know? What else would I love so much? Back and forth, back and forth my mind went, as if I were watching a tennis match.

"What in the world am I going to do?"

Once more, I tried to play. I played two tournaments at

the beginning of 1984 and lost in the first round of both of them. One of them was in Chicago. I saw a doctor there and decided I was going to play. I hadn't practiced in weeks and lost to Barbara Potter easily. Now that I think about that—and all of this—it was crazy. No one goes out and plays without practicing.

I had one more exhibition on my schedule. It was against Bettina Bunge at the Forum. I had not played in about a week because of an injury and was in the process of switching from a wooden racquet to a graphite model. When I got to the event, I opened my trunk and looked at the different racquets. I didn't know what to do. I was trying to change to graphite, yet I was much more confident playing with the old wooden racquet. Matt was with me and I asked him what he thought. What was I doing? I didn't have a clue. We chose the wooden racquet and I went out and lost in three sets.

I also gained two new injuries—hamstring and hip flexor pulls. I could barely make it off the court. I was lying on the training table, surrounded by a curtain and wracked with pain, when I blurted out, "I can't be injured! I have to play Hilton Head in two weeks!"

That was my frame of reference—play, play, play. Of course, there was absolutely no way I was playing Hilton Head.

I called my brother Jeff and asked him what I should do. He said I couldn't play anymore because I couldn't practice. That sounds logical, but I was so confused. Words that should have made sense didn't. Maybe I didn't want to hear them. But it didn't matter. I needed a break.

Although I always thought I was going to come back sometime soon, that was it, for all practical purposes. I was going full speed and had to jam on the brakes. There was no period of transition for me, like some of the other players have had, players like Chris, Billie Jean, Evonne. Comebacks were and are still possible, but little Tracy Austin, the teenage phenom, was finished—at least for a number of years.

I once read Dante: "In the middle of the journey of our

life, I came to myself within a dark wood where the straight way was lost."

That was me. I was doing so well and everything had gone so perfectly in my life and then I woke up one morning and was floundering. So much had been taken from me. I didn't have any goals. Goals? All my life was tennis. All my life, I had goals: for next year, for the next two years. For the next hour, for heaven's sake.

Now, I couldn't hit a tennis ball anymore.

# CHAPTER SIX

The limo dropped me off at the pier in Long Beach and by myself, I walked aboard the royal yacht *Britannia*. I was wearing a Grecian-style white crepe gown. I had not yet spotted the Queen of England, nor Prince Philip. At twenty, I was the youngest guest on board by at least twenty years.

In the crowd, I noticed Jerry Brown, the former governor of California. I perked up as he approached me. A familiar face, someone to talk to.

"Why are you here?" he asked.

"The queen invited me."

"What do you do?"

"I play tennis."

"Is that all you do?"

"Well, uh, basically, that's my career."

"Are you any good?"

"I guess I'm OK."

A waiter interrupted us and congratulated me on winning some recent tournament. That aroused Brown's curiosity.

"Have you ever won anything?"

"Well, a couple U.S. Opens."

Brown didn't change expression.

"Do you know any tennis players?" I asked him.

"Billie Jean King and Björn Borg," he said.

"Any others?"

"That's about it."

Astronomer Carl Sagan wandered by and began talking about the space stations we all will be living in someday. Brown became interested in that. Suddenly, James Zumberge, the USC president, came by and shook my hand.

"Oh, Tracy, we've been following your career for years," he said. "We saw you beat Billie Jean when we were at Wimbledon. You were spectacular!"

Jerry Brown finally showed some emotion. He realized who I was. His face turned red.

Soon, I met someone else—Prince Philip himself. Going through the receiving line, I first was introduced to the queen, then met the prince. When I shook his hand, he told me he'd always wanted to feel the calluses on a tennis player's hand.

When my career came to its sudden halt due to all those injuries, I was twenty-one, the age most people are when they are graduating from college and beginning their careers. But mine was on hold—at least until an aborted comeback attempt five years later.

I remember lying in bed in my home one morning in 1984, not really wanting to get up. It was so quiet and I felt so alone. I couldn't play tennis and I didn't know what I was going to do. I remember taking Matt to the airport and being so sad. First, because I was saying good-bye to my best friend and someone who was so supportive during the toughest times, and also because he was so lucky to be going off somewhere to play a tournament. I wanted to go play and realized it wasn't right around the corner.

As an athlete, I was used to being challenged. My life was exciting every day. I was used to traveling. Now, I was home all the time. It was hard for me to have nothing to do. I didn't want to be bored. People told me to relax and enjoy myself. I didn't want to relax. I called my friend Cari Horn. I listened to her plans for her upcoming wedding. I had no plans. I got off the phone and cried.

I was depressed for the first six months after leaving competitive tennis. I didn't know how to act. For me, it was such a shock, not being happy. I never had had things not go my way. I never had faced adversity. What do you do when things go wrong? I was searching for something, anything. To show how desperate I was, I called a popular L.A. radio psychologist and scheduled an appointment. He listened to me for an hour and a half, charged me six hundred dollars and told me I was confused. That bill confused me even more.

I know now I was both lucky and unlucky. The good part was I was young and inquisitive with some money in the bank. I was a millionaire several times over; my career winnings alone were $1.9 million. I had enough money to decorate my condo, which I did, right from the pages of magazines. I had enough money to travel. I didn't have to get a real job. I could do pretty much whatever I wanted with my time. And I found out I had wonderful friends. I met Tracy Tomson when I was dating her brother Shaun. She didn't know much about tennis, but she was the most outgoing, warm, and happy person I ever had met. Kathy Johnson, the former Olympic gymnast, understood what I was going through athletically. She and I talked a lot about getting out of sports and getting on with life.

The bad part of all this was I didn't want to have this much time on my hands. I was a tennis player and I wanted to play the game. My career had barely begun. I felt I had so much more to do and so much more of my game to develop. It was almost as if I had died on the court; so much was left undone.

I had not given up on tennis completely. If someone had told me in 1984 that I would not play until 1988, I would have thought that person was crazy. I was coming back in three months, I told myself. When those three months went by, I told myself it would be another three. I was playing when my back would allow it; Robert still was willing to help me; I was still seeing some doctors; I was still trying. It was one step forward, one step back. Injuries kept coming up—many different things. My body never got strong enough.

But deep down I knew that it wasn't going to happen overnight, and I needed to find something else to keep me busy. I became nostalgic for tennis and my career. Thank God, I said, for the opportunities I did have. I had won two U.S. Opens; I had traveled the world; I had played Chris seventeen times and won nine of them. I had had all that and no one could take it from me. Now, I simply was an old name with a new challenge. People knew me and liked me. I had contacts. I had social obligations. I did have a life to lead. But could I find something to interest me as much as tennis did?

To my surprise, I found out the answer was yes.

My looks had been a concern of mine when I was younger. The braces and the pigtails didn't make me feel very attractive. Until I met Matt Anger when I was eighteen, I dated very little. It is interesting to note, however, that high-school boys start asking you out after you've won your first Porsche.

Although we were both from California, I didn't meet Matt until the 1980 U.S. Open when a group of us were practicing. He was an accomplished junior player from northern California, which is a different section than southern California in junior tennis terms. I was smitten, but nothing came of it. Just another school-girl crush.

We ran into each other again at Wimbledon in 1981. Two of my friends, Shelly Solomon and Andrea Leand, were playing cards with him and I joined in and started talking. Pretty soon, he was calling my room and asking me out. The problem was, my whole family was in town and we were on our way to the Lonestar Cafe, a Bar-B-Q place we ate at every night that we were in London. And I do mean every night. We went there because the food was good; it was close, which meant we could walk and avoid taking cabs; and it was good luck, because John and I always played well after we ate there.

I invited Matt to join us. He was a trooper. He came along.

The next night, we went out alone and ended up talking in the lobby until six in the morning. My mother got concerned at about two o'clock when I hadn't come back to the room. I think she thought I was dead in a trash can somewhere. So she called my brother Jeff and he went down to the lobby to find us and report back that I was spotted and was alive.

John and I lost in the finals of the mixed doubles and Matt ended up winning the junior Wimbledon title that year. We went our separate ways but phoned every day and began dating seriously in the fall, when he began his freshman year at USC. He was perfect for me. We were young and naive and played tennis together and really were best friends. Everyone loved him. He was the perfect guy. If there had been something wrong with him, it would have been easy to let him go. But he was perfect. I asked myself, "Is this the only person who will come into my life? Is this the one?"

He treated me so well. He gave me a vanity license plate for my birthday that read, I M TAQEN. (The "K" already had been.) During the 1984 Olympics, he and I went to a Lionel Ritchie concert. Because of plantar fasciatis in my foot—the fascia is the sheath that surrounds the muscle in the arch, and when that tears, it aches—I couldn't walk. He carried me along. I was a basket case. I sat and cried. And he simply hugged me.

Matt wasn't intimidating to me. He was there during some of my good times, but more of my bad times. He put up with a lot. When I was injured, he would go out on a court with me, hit for ten minutes until I was in pain, and then leave with me. He was the only one who understood me. Everyone thought they couldn't help me because I was so confused. No one but Matt knew how to help. And even he couldn't do much. He knew what tennis meant to me, and he knew even he couldn't fill the void left by its absence.

Like almost every first boyfriend, he was meant to be in my life, but he wasn't destined to stay in it. We could have had a nice future together, but I was too young. I wanted more. There were so many people to see; so many places to visit. I needed to know who and what was out there.

It was very traumatic breaking up with him. Tears, phone calls, the works. And I think, to this day, I still love him. When I had my car accident in 1989, Matt, who by then was married, called me from Cincinnati, where he was playing a tournament. We talked for an hour and a half before he told me he was outside at a pay phone and it was an uncharacteristically chilly night and he was getting cold.

I'll never forget how we hung up.

"Send me a cigar when you have your first baby," I said.

"OK, and give me a call when you get married."

It was so sad. And so nice.

After that, I began seeing Shaun Tomson, the top-ranked surfer in the world and a Calvin Klein model. We dated about a year. I met Shaun at a Women's Sports Foundation dinner in San Francisco. He asked one of the other women athletes who I was. She told him.

"I thought Tracy Austin was a little girl," he said.

And I thought surfers were beach bums.

After that auspicious beginning, I traveled with him to Hawaii and England and cooked for him before big surfing competitions. It was fun to watch someone else get attention. Once, Shaun stood beside the ocean for twenty minutes, unable to move, because so many people wanted his autograph. I enjoyed watching him compete, too. I was glad to see he got nervous. He was anything but a beach bum. It turned out he went to college and was more well-read than I was. He and his family were from South Africa and had traveled a lot. They were very worldly.

More important, he told me I was pretty. For the longest time, I didn't believe him. I never thought I was. But you hear things often enough, and you begin to think they are true. He was turning thirty and he made me feel grown up.

Next was Greg Winfield, a model, actor, and part-time philosopher whom I dated for two or three months. I met him on a blind date. Kathrin Keil, a player on the circuit, was a friend of his and wanted to introduce us. She told me the only thing that was wrong in their friendship was they fought too much. That should have been a clue.

I loved to read throughout my life—mostly mysteries and romances—but Greg took me to the other side of the book-store—to philosophy, history, psychology. He made me see other sides of life. He told me sports were not life-and-death. Philosophy—now that was important. We discussed issues and argued a lot. He thought I was too intimidating. I don't think he liked strong women. The first time he came over, we talked for hours and hours. I had never met someone who had so much to say and so many ideas.

Greg was a real challenge to my values. No one really had made me think why I did the things I did—or didn't do the things I didn't do. I didn't do drugs, didn't drink much, didn't question authority—your basic Goody Two Shoes. But, at Cecelia Fernandez's engagement party, I watched him get into an argument about philosophy and make everyone mad. I told him an engagement party wasn't the time or the place for that serious a discussion.

One weekend, we drove up the coast to visit his family near San Francisco and on the way back, stopped in to see two psychologist friends of his in Big Sur. There, I was confronted by people smoking pot and using LSD—and unusual sleeping arrangements (two beds and six people). I thought everyone was strange and all I wanted to do was to get out of there. Was I right? I asked myself. Yes, I kept hearing back. I didn't want to do this and I told Greg so. So we left, right then and there. We drove for a while and then stopped to look for a hotel. There was none, so we pulled over on the side of the road. That night, I slept in the passenger seat of Greg's car on the side of the road. And Greg slept in the driver's seat. When dawn broke, we were on our way again. I couldn't get home fast enough.

Needless to say, Greg didn't last long after that.

Perhaps it was natural that I next seriously dated a family friend. I knew Bob Ruth, a commercial real estate developer, from our days at the Kramer Club. I grew up with his younger brother, Billy, and played tennis with his mother. Billy set us up on our first date.

This, too, was an eye-opening relationship, but in an entirely different way.

One day, I was supposed to drop him off at the airport for a trip to Miami to check on a racing boat he owned. He was driving my car when he suddenly pulled into the twenty-four-hour parking lot at LAX and informed me he had a plane ticket for me too.

"What are you talking about? I have to hit with Robert in an hour," I told him.

"Would you have fun going?" he asked me.

Of course the answer was yes, but I was so used to doing the practical thing that I couldn't fathom doing something like this. I called the club and told the person answering the phone that I didn't want to speak to Robert, who was supposed to give me my lesson, but I needed to cancel it. Robert would kill me, I thought.

Then I pulled my sweats on over my tennis clothes and walked into the airport. I finally got hold of my mother from Bob's cellular phone on the plane. I wanted to tell her what I was up to. I knew she would think it was funny. "Hey, Mom," I said. "Guess where I am." She knew how crazy Bob was, so she said, "I bet you're on the way to Florida." She thought it was a great idea. I went, watched power boat races, saw some friends, and had a terrific time.

Another time, we were involved with twenty other couples in a fun competition, which included a photo contest. Whichever couple had the most creative picture received the most points for their team, comprised of five couples. Our team wore different sports outfits—I was a water skier in a wet suit—and we jumped into the fountain by the Century Plaza Hotel and posed for our picture. All of a sudden, a group of Japanese tourists ran over and snapped more pictures of us. We got out of there quickly so we wouldn't get arrested.

I remember that my mother always was interested in what Bob and I were doing. She got a kick out of him. I did, too. But things didn't work out in the end with Bob. Perhaps we were too busy and too much alike. At one stretch, we went to black-tie dinners six out of twelve days. Bob is very successful and busy and he laughed that he was used to going to his own dinners and found my full life somewhat disarming. I understood; women like me, who have successful careers and don't need to rely on a boyfriend or husband for any financial help, can be a problem for men. It's so much more acceptable for a woman to tag along with a successful man than vice versa.

Bob and I are friends, as are most of my old boyfriends. This was the eighties, after all. Matt, Shaun, Greg, Bob—those were the first men in my life. At times, it got a little confusing. I told my dad when anyone called, "Don't say any names on the phone and don't make any specific comments." My Dad laughed when I finally dated someone who carried a briefcase. It was Bob.

I met a couple of men in the strangest ways. One day, I had visited Tracy Tomson at the surf shop she and her brother owned on Wilshire Boulevard. I left and was driving down Wilshire in my Mercedes when two men in a Rolls Royce stopped beside me at a light and said, "Bet I can beat you at tennis."

"I bet you can," I said, and pulled away as the light turned green.

Next light. "Hey, what's your name?" one of the guys asked.

"I'm not telling you," I said. At this point, I thought they knew who I was. I was wrong.

Next light. "Come on, what's your name?"

"Tracy," I said.

"What's your number?"

I didn't want to give it out, so I quickly rattled off Tracy's number at the shop and drove away.

A few minutes later, Tracy Tomson got a phone call at work.

"I'm looking for Tracy," the man said.

"That's me," Tracy said, with her distinctive South African accent.

"So, are you going to play tennis with me?" he asked.

"Who are you? What are you talking about?" she said.

"I just saw you on Wilshire Boulevard in the black Mercedes and you gave me this number."

She laughed and said, "Oh, no, that's my friend, whose name also is Tracy."

They started to talk to figure out what had happened. She asked if he knew who I was. He had no idea.

But he told her he wanted to take me out to Valentino's, a restaurant in L.A., for dinner.

When I returned to Tracy's shop, she told me what had happened and we laughed. She tried to convince me to go to dinner and I said, "No way. I don't even know him."

"It's safe," she said. "You'll meet him there. You only live once."

I went. His name was Loay Nazer. He was from Saudi Arabia and his father was involved with OPEC. He was fascinating to talk to because he came from a different culture. He told me he was going to have an arranged marriage, as was the custom of his family. We said our good-byes at the restaurant and started a nice friendship that night.

A couple years later, Scott Holt and I saw Loay at the Volvo tennis tournament. He was with a woman. Sure enough, the arranged marriage had taken place.

In keeping with this theme of "You only live once," I met another man, Scott Irwin, in a similar way in Houston. I had flown in for a corporate obligation and taken a cab to my hotel. A few minutes after I checked in and got to my room, the phone rang. It was a man who had spotted me in traffic, had followed my cab, and had come into the lobby to meet me.

It took a lot of convincing before I would come down to the lobby to meet Scott, and I found him to be very funny and nice. After we talked for a while, I said I was going to the Galleria, where I wanted to try on dresses at North Beach Leather. He said he would take me. The salesclerks thought he was my boyfriend or husband and kept asking him what he thought of me in each dress. Boy, did we laugh about that.

I also had a few celebrity dates. Not many, but the ones I had were hilarious, mostly because I still had these schoolgirl values. What was a nice girl like me doing in places like this?

I met Alan Thicke, the TV actor, at a celebrity tournament in Florida. He invited me to his house in Los Angeles to play tennis. The day I came his sister answered the door and instructed me to go upstairs. He yelled out for me to come into the bedroom. "Come into the bathroom," he then said.

I gingerly peeked my head around the door and there he was, bathing. He acted as if a conversation from the tub with someone he barely knew was the most normal thing in the world. I got embarrassed. Obviously, he didn't. I talked fast and made a quick exit. After that interesting beginning, Alan became a good friend. I invited him to my twenty-fifth birthday party—where one hundred fifty guests all wore something pink, my favorite color—and he has played in my charity tournament.

Then there was Rob Lowe. Yes, Rob Lowe. I met him in

Toronto at a celebrity tennis tournament. We went from one party to another and he kept bugging me and pretty soon he was holding my hand and inviting me to his hotel room.

To sum up that one: Yes, he tried; no, I didn't.

There have been dozens of famous people who have passed through my life, some I've met for an evening, some for a couple days during charity events, others I bump into once or twice a year at some special event. When you're famous, it's often easy to lose perspective, but I never did, because when I look back, I always felt lucky and honored to be a part of these functions. I've been to the White House about ten times and have been invited to many Hollywood functions. Sometimes I had to laugh at what I saw; other times, I was extremely impressed by a famous person.

Because of Wimbledon, the royal family liked me. They came to Los Angeles on occasion, and I frequently got an invitation. The Duke and Duchess of Kent were promoting English art in America at the Los Angeles County Museum of Art. Off I went. The duchess was a very kind, down-to-earth person. She told me she had switched to playing tennis in the same brand of shoes I wore, hoping it would help her game. Elizabeth Taylor was there, too. What struck me about her was her soft, beautiful skin and gorgeous features. She was exquisite. But then my eyes wandered to the Rembrandts on the wall behind her. They captivated me. The eyes in the paintings seemed so real. I wanted to linger there forever and take it all in. Seeing those paintings reminded me of how much I missed, that becoming great in something meant giving up so much in other areas.

At the Night of 100 Stars, a charity event in New York, there was a kaleidoscope of images. The one hundred stars turned into about three hundred; everyone was there for their moment in the sun, to be introduced on stage. Joan Collins came, very intent on showing off the rock she had just received from Peter Holm. Some of the women, like Raquel Welch, refused to come in for the rehearsal because they felt above it all. Howard Cosell teased me about having a crush on Miami Dolphin quarterback Dan Marino, who of course came by right at that moment. Naturally, Cosell kept right on talking about it. I met figure skater Peggy Fleming in the makeup room and we got along great from the start. She and I wandered around, mingling, saying hello to everyone. We were like little kids. You might as well have fun at something like that. She and I have been together at other functions, including the Sudafed Symphony of Sports in Vail, Colorado, where I did a tennis clinic and she skated, of course, and a nice friendship has developed.

The Reagans—Californians like me—invited me to their home-away-from-home, the White House, for their "Just Say No" tournament every year, beginning in 1985. (Now it's held at the Riviera Tennis Club.) Even now when I see Mrs. Reagan, she always pulls me aside and asks how I'm doing. I saw her at an AIDS research benefit run by Paul Michael Glaser's wife, Elizabeth, then again at her charity tennis event in October 1991. She feels comfortable with me now. I look at her and President Reagan and sometimes feel sorry for them. It must be hard for them to go to event after event, not knowing people, being stared at, and having bodyguards around.

I'll never forget the time I was at the White House in 1988 and President Reagan kept four or five of us in stitches for quite a while telling Gorbachev jokes. He was so happy telling stories. In October 1991, I was at a cocktail party in his huge office in Century City, with one of the best views of Los Angeles, and saw the bullet that John Hinckley shot at him. It's encased in glass with a plaque that reads THIS IS IT.

I also saw a thoughtful side of President Reagan at a Ford corporate meeting in Phoenix in 1989, after his presidency was over. He made a speech, while I was there to give a tennis clinic. He was told his plane was going to be held up due to mechanical problems and, right away, he said to one of his assistants, "Call Nancy and tell her I'll be late."

I was invited to play at the White House with President

Bush's son Marvin, who is a neighbor of my brother Jeff's in Alexandria, Virginia. Marvin gave me a tour of the family quarters after we played, and what struck me most was the bulletproof window glass that was about a foot thick. Other than that, the quarters seemed just the way Mrs. Bush would have them. It was a very homey place.

The AIDS research benefit is the biggest charity event I go to in Los Angeles every year. It draws such stars as Robin Williams, Whoopie Goldberg, Lloyd and Jeff Bridges, and boxer George Foreman: about seventy-five celebrities all together. It's a carnival; we celebs run booths while children try to win prizes. I worked a booth for an hour, giving balls to kids to throw through loops. It was a mess; I had balls all over the floor. The money the families pay to send their kids to the carnival helps support the charity. It's great to see busy celebrities give their time back in that way.

I met Brooke Shields at the White House in 1985; she was so sweet and bright and easy to talk to right away. We talked about what it was like for both of us to deal with so much at such young ages. There are very few people who understand what my life was like; she did, because she had the same life. We discussed how we tried to stay normal while some people around us acted differently toward us.

And I even did a TV show: *Mork and Mindy,* in 1982. I was Mork's tennis coach. I said my line and Robin Williams went on a five-minute rampage of impressions and jokes on McEnroe, Nastase, and Connors that had me doubled over with laughter. We reshot the scene.

Later I saw him as a surprise stand-up comic in New York. People called out subjects from the audience; what amazed me was how he thought so quickly on the spot. What an intelligent man.

I hung out with other athletes as well. I became friends with Indy race car driver Danny Sullivan. We met in a strange place. At Victoria Principal's celebrity tournament at La Costa in 1985, Linda Jenner, Bruce's wife, and I went into the ladies' room. All of a sudden, we saw Danny and Alan Nierob, Danny's public relations man, in the bathroom with us. They just wandered in to be silly.

With a start like that, you know you're going to become friends. We spent time together that weekend. Next thing I knew, Bruce Jenner was flying me in his private plane to Phoenix to watch Danny race there. As we drove in from the airport, Bruce floored it, then pulled out the emergency brake and we did a 360-degree spin. On the highway. All these people are crazy, I decided, but in a good way. They just like scary things more than I do. Plus, they can't be that crazy or they all would be dead by now.

I went to Long Beach to watch Danny race there and had an accident of my own. Danny had just won the pole at the Long Beach Grand Prix and was driving Alan and me in a golf cart around the grounds by the track to a press conference. He didn't slow down at a turn and dumped both Alan and me onto the road. I flew out of the cart and landed on my head—and Alan fell on me. Danny picked us up and took us to the Penske trailer—where we had just been—and I received seven stitches in the back of my head. I had blood all over my white blouse. It was quite a pit stop. I still have a bump on my head to remind me. Nice driving, Danny.

Right after that, Danny took me to his hotel room a hundred yards away so I could rest. I had a hood on my head to cover the blood and the mess and he had his arm around me. I told him to tell his girlfriend, Julie, that it was just me. It had to look like he was sneaking a woman into his room.

Aside from that disaster, I loved being around other athletes. I enjoyed seeing how they prepared for their competition. I have a great deal of respect for them and what they do. I love talking about their technique. I once chatted with Johnny Miller at Pebble Beach about how he prepared for a round of golf. We were both there for a corporate outing for *Sports Illustrated* clients. He played golf with some and I played tennis with a few others. He got me out on the golf course and watched me swing and try to putt. I've attempted golf a couple times, but I'm not any good. I didn't even know how to hold the golf club or where my feet were supposed to be. My problems with the game gave me an eye-opening appreciation of what tennis must be like for beginners.

What's funny, though, is that I've done a golf video. Bob Mann, a golf pro, invited athletes of different levels to try to learn, and he'd make a videotape at the same time. He had me, Oscar Robertson, Arthur Ashe, and Bart Conner, among others. In the video, I did well. Bob told me I could be good. But I haven't given it any more time.

I met Herschel Walker in Arizona, where we were doing a Foster-Grant sunglasses commercial, and watched him do one thousand situps. Well, I didn't watch every single one, but I got the idea. He is in incredible shape and eats just one meal a day and said he never has lifted weights. Every professional athlete has to be so fine-tuned mentally. Not too many people in the real world know that level of intensity and concentration.

I was with athletes all day at the Live Aid concert in Philadelphia. Actually, I've gone to quite a few events like that. I really enjoy doing those things. They keep me involved and allow me to see friends and meet new people since I don't play on the circuit anymore. I made a couple-paragraph speech at the concert on behalf of the athletes who were there; Mark Gastineau made one, too. There we were in front of more than one hundred thousand people. I wouldn't have minded playing tennis in front of them, but speaking before them was nerve-wracking.

Once in Palm Springs at a Ford corporate outing, I accompanied the car dealers to a function where Barry Manilow was singing. He asked for a volunteer to join him for one song and I ended up on stage with him.

"Are you a car dealer?" he asked me.

"No," I said.

"Are you married to a car dealer?"

"No," I said.

"Are you even married?" he asked.

"No, but I do have four kids." Everyone started laughing.

That confused Barry so much that we broke into a song. I joined him in singing, "Can't Smile Without You," but I didn't sing very loudly. I let him handle it.

I've also gotten to know David Robinson of the San Antonio Spurs. Jeff is one of his agents and the three of us once went bodysurfing in the waves off Ixtapa, Mexico. It got so rough that he told me to grab on to his neck and ride the wave in. He became my surfboard.

I'm so impressed with David—especially off the court. He's so well adjusted to his fame.

My main activity when I wasn't playing tennis was to, well, play tennis. Pro-ams, dozens of them, corporate outings, exhibitions, clinics. I was paired with everyone from Peter Jennings to Farrah Fawcett to Bill Cosby. Some were fun, some were trying. But everyone had some redeeming quality.

I hope I'm not embarrassing anyone, but of all the celebrity amateurs I played, these were some of the best, in some kind of order:

Bill Cosby—Open—great serve and volleyer, crowd-pleaser.

Kenny Rogers—Open—brings his own pro with him, pretty complete game.

Robert Duvall—Open—so tough he swears at the ball boys, very competitive.

Rick Barry—Open—very difficult top-spin serve, could have been great at tennis.

Bruce Jenner—A-plus—decathletes can become great tennis players, wanted to improve badly.

Steve Garvey—A-plus—incredibly consistent at net.

Peter Jennings—A—a real fun guy on the court, fluid serve.

Chad Everett—A-minus—a real veteran, and it shows.

Gene Wilder—B-plus—loved him as Willie Wonka, steady as a backboard.

Danny Sullivan—B—more aggressive on the race track than on the court, good foot speed.

Alan Thicke—B—always gets the ball back, loves the game.

Sidney Poitier—B—nice, fluid game, fun to watch.

Kirk Cameron—B—ball girls love him.

Johnny Carson—B—fellow L.A. Strings draft choice years ago, doubles partner at thirteen in Las Vegas.

Pat Boone—B—great at carrying a racquet and a tune.

Wayne Gretzky—B—looks like Björn Borg out there, eh? Could have been good at any sport.

Lloyd Bridges—B—beat him when I was nine, a great sport, very consistent.

Merv Griffin—B—very funny, great jokes, good game shows—*Jeopardy* is my favorite.

John Forsythe—B—comes to my charity event every year, a real trouper.

Sean Connery—B-minus—kicked me off court in Aspen, so gets a minus. (Just kidding.)

Charlton Heston—C—overcomes bad knees with nice strokes.

Bart Conner—C—an Olympic gymnast with a perfect 10.0 from the U.S. judge, improving quickly.

Chuck Norris—C—took his first lessons before my charity event, lightning speed.

And the top two women:

Cathy Lee Crosby—Open—played as a junior, very good.

Farrah Fawcett—A-plus—love the two-handed backhand, steady baseline game.

While I'm on the subject, it can be difficult to be a sports star or a celebrity. You do so many charity events or public appearances that it sometimes becomes tough for even the nicest people to smile. But I shouldn't complain. I could be Wilt Chamberlain.

I saw Wilt at a wedding in 1991 and realized his problem. He couldn't be just a guest at the wedding; he had to be Wilt. People came up to him all day and asked for his autograph and took photos with him. He obliged, but I really felt sorry for him. Because he's so tall and recognizable, he can never be "normal."

At the Manhattan Beach tournament a few years ago, I was sitting next to Wilt. (We have been friends for quite a while, but, no, I was not one of the twenty thousand women. Not even close.) A woman came up and said she admired him and wanted an autograph for her son. Wilt said that he would do it once the tiebreaker we were watching ended.

I watched the woman walk away—she never came back—and I could imagine her saying, "God, what an ass that guy is." In that instant, I'll bet her whole image of Wilt Chamberlain changed for good.

Yet, sometimes fans and autograph-seekers push you to the limit. At Wimbledon one year, I was walking from the locker room to the tearoom and got mobbed by people wanting my autograph. I was wearing a white angora sweater that day. I asked everyone to move back, promising I would sign them all. But the people didn't move away. In fact, they moved forward and started to squeeze around me. All of a sudden, I felt a pen run down my back. I pulled the sweater around so I could see the back, and, sure enough, a huge line had ruined it.

In other ways, the years following my departure from the circuit took me far from tennis.

"This is my time to be free and have fun," I told the *Los Angeles Times* in October 1987.

My father made an astute observation to *Times* reporter Irene Garcia: "Everyone needs a time to have no commitments, a time where there's nothing you really have to do. For most people, it's a childhood phase with no responsibility. For Tracy, that phase has been the last four years, and it's been great for her."

I went on a cruise to Mexico with three girlfriends: Kathy Johnson, Tracy Tomson, and our friend Jackie Harris, who was one of my producers in London when I worked for *Good Morning America*. I have a photo from that vacation on a table at home.

I met Kathy at a Women's Sports Foundation media training course, where she was my roommate. The first night, we stayed up until five in the morning just talking. I realized she and I agreed on everything—especially on how so much emphasis had been placed on our sports and how we were making the adjustment to outside life. I was so glad to meet someone through sports who agreed with me on life outside sports. We also agreed on how wonderful sports had been for us—the qualities we acquired and the experiences and self-esteem we gained. I haven't found that many people I could relate to in that way.

Tracy is Shaun's sister and the best thing to come out of that relationship—only joking, Shaun. She plays tennis horribly—which I love. She's just a great person, takes everything in, and wants to learn. I look at her as a role model for how to enjoy life.

Both Kathy and Tracy have traveled with me on my TV assignments. Kathy went to a U.S. Open with me in 1986. Every morning, we walked through Central Park, then she went with me to the National Tennis Center and watched the matches all day. And every night, we went dancing with a group of people we had gathered at the tournament: players, agents, friends.

One night, I was on a date and he came back to the room Kathy and I shared. We turned on a movie in the room and I promptly fell asleep. Kathy entertained him, saying, "Don't take this personally. She falls asleep watching movies all the time."

Tracy went to London with me in 1986. I never worried about her having a good time. Every night when I was done, she'd tell me about the ten new friends she had spent the day with.

At that time in my life, I went shopping; boy, did I go

shopping. I traveled just for fun and went to other sporting events. I decorated my home. I got into gardening. Reporters stopped calling for interviews, and I loved it. When they did call, I even refused to do a couple interviews with *Sports Illustrated* and *Tennis* magazine. I had absolutely nothing to say.

Also during that time, I remember always thinking I should be doing something else. I wanted more. I wished I could find another passion like tennis. I kept a diary then (and still do) and I wanted to fill the pages with wonderful events. Every day had to be full and interesting. I didn't want to waste any time at all. I took classes in real estate, photography, and pottery. My childhood friend Cari, who didn't play tennis seriously and was married at twenty-one and now has two kids and a white-picket fence, said I was making up for lost time. I think she was right.

Yet, something still was missing. I had too much time. The toughest part was it was so open-ended. I had no goals: I was striving for nothing.

In June 1986, I got a call saying that *Good Morning America* needed a correspondent to do interviews from Wimbledon. It was a Thursday. I had to leave Saturday because Wimbledon started on Monday. I jumped at the chance.

I had had other infrequent television opportunities. As I was talking to reporters about defaulting at the 1983 Wimbledon, an NBC producer called the press room and asked if I wanted to work as a color commentator for their broadcasts. I was thrown into it totally unprepared and didn't know what I was doing, but I tried. I had been seeded number four in the tournament, so I didn't really have my heart and mind into the TV job. While commentating the final between Martina and Andrea, I wanted to be out there. I wasn't removed enough from the game to give an accurate account. I did analysis and color, no interviews. I did OK. I raced back to tennis as soon as my back would allow it.

This time around, in 1986, Chris was my first interview.

We talked in the backyard of the house she owned with John Lloyd at Wimbledon, and I was surprised that I had dozens of things I wanted to ask her. I knew her life and felt very comfortable with the microphone. I just asked questions I was really curious about. I wasn't masquerading as a TV reporter, as I had been in 1983. Now, this was my job.

Billie Jean King gave me a nickname years ago: "Why?" She said she gave me that name because I loved to ask so many questions. She was right. (She also called me Baby Cakes, but that was because I was so little when I was playing.)

I started to realize that we athletes can be challenging interviews sometimes. Mary Joe Fernandez, fourteen at the time, was so shy she gave me one-word answers. She didn't mean to be difficult, she was just being sweet and nervous and fourteen. She reminded me of myself. She left me hanging after every question. Back to you, Joan.

Boris Becker was two hours late for his interview and we almost missed our deadline. Jimmy Connors, whom I knew through my brother Jeff when I was a little girl, nearly cracked me up on the air by teasing me about who I was dating and telling me dirty jokes seconds before we were to go on.

I loved the work that summer. It was the first thing I had done that gave me the same kind of adrenaline rush that tennis did. And yet it was bizarre, because I really felt removed from the tennis world. Being the interviewer, not the interviewee, really put in bold ink that I was not playing anymore. There I was, interviewing Martina about her tennis career, and it hit me that she's six years older than I am. I was twenty-three, she was twenty-nine; she was still out there playing and I was not.

I went back to Wimbledon for *Good Morning America* the next year and the highlight of that trip was a fire at the ABC studios in London. I was caught in traffic—someone parked in someone else's spot and the ensuing argument held up traffic for twenty minutes—and came up to the building in time to hear the fire bell going off.

While everyone was fleeing because of the smoke, my

producer, Teri Lickstein, was dragging me into the building. "Come on, we're live!" she yelled.

There was smoke everywhere. We ran up four flights of stairs, I sat down, put my earpiece in with thirty seconds to go, took a deep breath, and coughed.

"So, Tracy, tell us about today's play at Wimbledon," Charlie Gibson began.

I ended up giving one of my better reports. I loved the pressure. And I loved the feeling when I was finished, the same kind of high you get after a good match.

In 1990, I was at the U.S. Open for some promotional work for sponsors, which I do every year. The people at USA Network asked if I would come on the air with them and be a guest commentator. I said yes. They must have liked what I did because they kept asking me back. And I loved it.

The day of the women's final, I played a pro-am with some corporate clients in the morning. I showered and threw on black bicycle shorts and a black T-shirt. They told me the wardrobe person would be around to take care of me for the show.

Well, she had gone home for the day, so there I was, about to go on TV in bicycle shorts.

I looked over at Billie Jean, who was scheduled to go on the air, too. She was wearing a nice blouse and blazer.

"Hey, Billie, how about if I grab your blazer?"

She gave it to me, I crossed my legs on the set and it looked like I was wearing a short skirt. On went the cameras; we were on the air. Such ingenuity.

I soon learned that television superseded everything, even the threat of electrocution. I worked for NBC at Wimbledon in 1991, and fellow commentator Dick Enberg and I were on our NBC set on the roof at Wimbledon, hooked up, ready to talk with some local TV stations back in the United States via satellite.

The skies opened, as they often do at Wimbledon, and it poured. I looked at Dick. He never stopped talking.

Dick is such a professional. He writes his own stuff and then says it with the greatest of ease. He used to carry three-by-five-inch index cards on all the players before everything became computerized. At Wimbledon in 1991, Bud Collins found the cards and Dick gave me mine, tattered and worn as it was.

At that same Wimbledon, Jimmy Connors and I did a satellite hookup with thirty cities back in the States. We had to talk to each station separately and, after a while, we got punchy. Jimmy was saying something about women's tennis and I said, "Jimmy, you didn't watch that match. You get bored with women's tennis."

"You're right," he said. We both laughed.

At least he's honest.

Later that year, at the Open, Vitas Gerulaitis and I were both working for USA Network. They wanted us to do a piece starting in the respective locker rooms and moving to the stadium. Walking and talking at the same time on TV can be very, very difficult.

The first time, we had to go through a door and Vitas pushed it so hard it bounced back and hit me in the face.

Take Two: He opens the door without incident—and steps on my foot.

Take Three: We finally get through the door, turn to look at each other, and instead of saying our lines, stare at each other for a split-second and then crack up.

Holding the trophy I had worked so hard to recapture. I had been out four months earlier in the year with a bad back, and people were already writing me off.
PHOTOGRAPH BY CAROL L. NEWSOM

Martina Navratilova, Billie Jean King, Chris Evert, and me in Palm Springs. The only other Number One–ranked women since the computer rankings started in 1973 were Margaret Court Smith, Steffi Graf, and Monica Seles. PHOTOGRAPH BY CAROL L. NEWSOM

ABOVE LEFT: With Tom Selleck, President and Mrs. Reagan, and Pam Shriver in 1985 at Mrs. Reagan's Just Say No charity event at the White House. Someone had just said something funny, and it probably was Pam.   *The Washington Post*

RIGHT: My favorite photograph, because I look peaceful and content. This was taken in 1985, at a time when I had started to find more balance in my life.   PHOTOGRAPH BY LARRY ARMSTRONG, *Los Angeles Times Magazine*

Giving Peter Jennings a few tips in Hilton Head, South Carolina. He has a great sense of humor and learned quickly.   PHOTOGRAPH BY CAROL L. NEWSOM

My first interview for *Good Morning America* in Chris Evert's backyard at her house at Wimbledon, 1986. I felt comfortable because I knew the subject well.

With Jeff, my brother and agent; Cari Horn (*seated across from me*); and Jackie Harris, my producer in London for *Good Morning America*, in the remodeled tearoom at Wimbledon. This room is more functional, but I loved the old wicker furniture and flowered pillows of the other.

ABOVE: With Sugar Ray Leonard and my friend Tracy Tomson on the balcony of the Wimbledon tearoom in 1987. I sat next to Sugar Ray during Martina's final, and he was a nervous wreck.

RIGHT: With Tracy Tomson, my fun-loving best friend, outside Martina's rented house fifty yards from Wimbledon. We had just celebrated with her after her 1987 victory. I was working with *Good Morning America*, and Tracy and I had the greatest time in London.

Preparing to interview Martina after her 1987 Wimbledon victory. She is always very honest with her answers.

Getting silly with Chris Evert (*to my left*), Andy Mill, and other players in the French Quarter during a tournament in New Orleans    PHOTOGRAPH BY CAROL L. NEWSOM

With my brother John during Team Tennis in New Jersey. I was happy we played on the same team and could support each other.

With Tracy Tomson, Mom, good friend Kathy Johnson, and my physical therapist, Joe, in the hospital two days after surgery. I was feeling so sick, but Tracy and Kathy stayed with me all day to give my mom a rest. The doctors grafted bone from my right hip into the outside of my right knee.

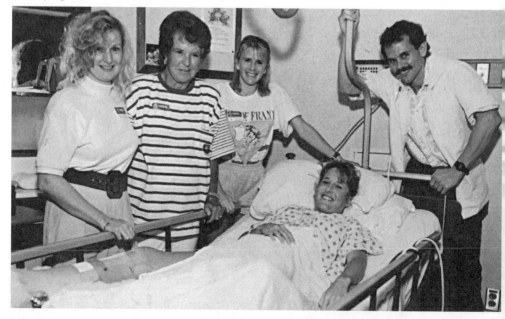

In October 1990 at the dinner for Nancy Reagan's annual charity event, now held in Los Angeles. Mrs. Reagan always takes time to talk to my boyfriend, Scott, and me.
PHOTOGRAPH BY MIKE GUASTELLA

LEFT: With my boyfriend, Scott, at the NBC Compound at the 1991 Wimbledon Championships. My workday usually lasted about twelve hours. ABOVE: With Dick Enberg at Wimbledon on the Centre Court roof. The outside courts and the town of Wimbledon are in the background. It looks sunny, but typical of English weather, it rained fifteen minutes later.

I love tennis and I love to talk, so I loved my job as commentator for NBC at Wimbledon in 1991. I had a great time working with Jimmy Connors, who had me laughing the whole time.

BELOW LEFT: My living room at my annual Christmas party. I'm with my best friend throughout high school, Cari Horn Utnehmer. She gave some balance to my life during the first years on the circuit.

RIGHT: With another of my best friends, Kathy Johnson, a gymnastics silver medalist in the 1984 Olympics. We met at an athletic function, hit it off right away, and it was a blessing to have her support and knowledge during the toughest times in my career.

With Scott, the boat captain, and our guide, deep-sea fishing off Guam in December 1991. Believe me, I didn't know where Guam was when I was asked to do some tennis clinics and an exhibition there. We had a super time and caught about ten fish. Man, that's a lot of work pulling them in!

Christmas, 1991. *Top row, left to right*: George (Dad), Brooke (Doug's wife), John, Doug, Erin (Doug's daughter), Jeff. *Bottom row*: Christopher (John's son), Karen (John's wife), Westley (Doug's son), me, Brian (Doug's son), Mrs. Hodges (grandmother), Pam, Denise (Jeff's wife), Kelly (Jeff's daughter). Jeanne (Mom) is seated on the floor. PHOTOGRAPH BY DEL LITTLE

# CHAPTER SEVEN

It was August 3, 1989, a beautiful, sunny Thursday in the New York area. The day fit my mood. I was healthy and playing tennis again, getting ready for the 1989 U.S. Open by playing Team Tennis in New Jersey with my brother John. I was finally coming back after five long years. What a tremendous feeling that was.

I pulled out of the parking lot at the Hilton in Short Hills, New Jersey, at about ten o'clock, on my way to get preventative ultrasound treatment on my foot, which had been sore, with Dr. David Jacobs before my match that night.

I approached the intersection to the JFK Parkway in my car to make a left turn to get on the highway. From about fifty yards away, I could see the left-turn arrow was on. I kept going.

Then, in a split-second, in the intersection, I saw him. Out of the corner of my eye, a van was in my side window, right on top of me, running the red light. I saw a flash of blond hair, a dark van, and then . . . nothing. My body checked out. I have no recollection of the accident or spinning or falling out the car door when it flew open and the seat belt released.

I woke up upside down. My back was on the ground, my legs were up on the seat and I was staring at the sky. My car was turned completely around, sixty-five feet from the intersection. I was in so much pain I could hardly move. My neck. My back. I strained to look around. Suddenly, a face appeared in front of me. A wonderful man was standing over me. I found out only his first name, Dan. He saw the accident and while no one else stopped, he did. He said later he started to come over to me and stopped for a moment, because he was afraid of seeing what was over there. But he kept coming anyway, and found me.

I don't know if he shook me awake or I just woke up; all I knew was when I woke up, he was there.

"Calm down, calm down," he was telling me.

"I'm paralyzed," I screamed. "I can't move!" I was hysterical.

"Don't move," Dan said, putting his arm on my shoulder. "Don't move."

"I'm paralyzed!" While I was screaming I was paralyzed, I was kicking my legs like a little child. But nothing registered in those first scary moments. The information that I could in fact move my legs wasn't going to my brain quickly enough. I had so much pain in my back, I couldn't be paralyzed, but fear grabbed hold of me and I didn't know what was wrong.

I noticed blood dripping off my hands and legs. I wiped my face. Blood was on my sleeve. I had cuts all over.

I started to pinch my legs.

"Am I going to be OK?" I yelled out. Then I started calling out for my brother John. "Get John!" I yelled. "He's in the hotel."

Pretty soon John was running up to me, grabbing my hand. He told me later he was walking toward the accident from our hotel, but when he saw my car, totally destroyed, he started running.

The paramedics told him to calm down and not scare me.

"I'm paralyzed!" I screamed to him.

"Tracy, you're killing my hand," he said. "You're not paralyzed."

Then I focused on my back. "My back's broken!" I yelled.

They strapped me to a board and put me in a neck brace up to my nose. All of a sudden, tennis was the farthest thing from my mind. You're driving a car one minute and the next minute, you're mangled. It was so unreal, it was like a dream. Everyone says that, but it's true. This couldn't be happening to me.

They put me in the ambulance and the guy who hit me was sitting there, too. I couldn't see him, but I could hear him crying. He had a broken arm, I think they said. I don't know if he was crying from the pain or from what he had just done.

I got to the hospital and John and I had to wait in the emergency room forever, it seemed, to see a doctor. The X-ray machine was being used, so I just lay there on a gurney, crying. I had a cut on my leg so a nurse came by and gave me seven stitches. Otherwise, I was hysterical.

"My back is getting worse," I cried to John.

"It's stiffening up," he told me.

It was an hour before they took me in for X rays. They took pictures of everything imaginable. It's amazing I don't glow in the dark. The technician came out and I asked him how it looked. He said he wasn't supposed to say anything, but that it looked good. My back and my neck were not broken.

"I love you," I said to him.

"You don't have to be that drastic," he said.

I was thrilled. I was so scared that I would not be able to walk again. I ached like no pain I had had before.

Then they stuck me in a Magnetic Resonance Imaging machine, which would be a very scary experience for a completely healthy person. It was totally claustrophobic. It's like going into a tunnel with hammering in your ears. The machine makes such a loud noise. You must lie still inside it for a half hour to forty-five minutes. The nurses told me if I panicked, I should yell out to them. I still get chills thinking about that machine.

After the tests and doctors and nurses poking around, I was told I had a bruised heart and bruised spleen from the seat belt and a sprained back that would require a few days in bed. I was sore all over, but, otherwise, I was fine. How lucky I was. I looked at myself and saw a purple line running diagonally from my left shoulder to my right hip, and then another line across my stomach. The seat belt left its mark. Thank God for that. Without it, they told me, I would have been dead.

They wheeled me into a room and finally put me in a bed. At about five o'clock, I gingerly got out of bed to go to the bathroom. I tried to stand. Something was wrong, terribly wrong. I looked down at my right knee and saw the worst swelling I had ever seen. And the pain. Unbelievable. The doctors had missed it. They had been worried about life-threatening things. For seven hours, they and I had not been aware of a shattered bone below the knee. I must have had so much pain elsewhere, I hadn't even noticed that.

I called the nurse and pointed to my knee. "I think something's wrong," I said.

John had been at the hospital with me all day, as had my boyfriend, Wolf Mack. John left late in the afternoon, completely drained, and played and won his men's doubles match with Bill Scanlon that night. My mother was calling all the time. We had told her not to come, that I was going to be fine.

At ten-thirty that evening, the doctor came in.

"So I guess you're going to have surgery on your knee, a couple screws and a couple plates," he said.

"What?" That was the first I heard that my leg was crushed, just below the knee.

I called my mother. She said she was coming out, but until we knew how serious it was, I told her to wait.

Another doctor came in. He avoided eye contact, but suggested I have the surgery in either New York or Los Angeles. I knew Doctors Robert Kerlan and Frank Jobe at Centinela

Hospital near Los Angeles, so that was the place, I said. I found out a Dr. Robert Chandler was the fracture and trauma specialist there. He was the man I would see.

Once again, I was reduced to tears, but this time I was alone in a hospital bed. I thought I was OK. I thought I'd be out a week or so and then back in time for the Open. Now this. I wouldn't be ready for this Open, or maybe any other Open. My knee was crushed.

As I lay in the darkness that night, I kept hearing two awful words in my head: *Why me? Why me?*

The phone rang again. It was my mother. I sobbed to her, then she helped me collect my thoughts. "You know, Tracy," she said, "'Why you?' a lot of things. Why did you have the talent to win the U.S. Open at sixteen? And your determination—why were you given that? Why did you get the strength to achieve so many things? Don't you think your sister would have loved to win the U.S. Open? Or to meet the President? Or the Queen?"

My trip to California for surgery was very painful. I was on a stretcher and took an ambulance for my ride to the airport, then was carried onto the plane on the stretcher. I had to sit in the same seat in the plane for five hours, unable to move. I sat across three seats, with pillows behind my back and under my leg. I hardly drank anything because I couldn't go to the bathroom. I hurt so much, I never even thought about having to go.

I got back to Los Angeles Sunday and took an ambulance to Centinela Hospital Medical Center in Inglewood. There, they gave me a huge room and let my mom stay with me on a pull-out bed. The room was full of flowers and balloons and cards from players, family, and friends—that cheered me for a few minutes before reality sunk in again.

My surgery was scheduled for eleven o'clock Monday morning, August 7. I was going through the *Los Angeles Times* that morning to take my mind off the surgery and was shocked to read of the death of Stacy Toran of the Los Angeles

Raiders, who was killed in a car accident the day before. He was a great player in the prime of his career, making all kinds of money and seemingly doing everything right, except he was driving drunk without a seat belt. His car hit the curb and flew into the air before hitting a tree. He was thrown from the car and died of head injuries. I think about him even now. Two car accidents, two athletes, and I was the lucky one.

I was in surgery for five hours. The doctors grafted bone from my right hip and used it to rebuild below my knee-cap—the tibia plateau—so my thigh bone (femur) could once again fit in place. They put in just one screw and no plates. It's still there and it hurts like heck when I bump it, which I do about once a day.

The most amazing thing was, when I awoke from surgery, my leg was moving. They put my leg in a Constant Passive Motion machine, which moves the joint back and forth to keep the knee from stiffening while it heals. I had to be in that machine thirteen hours a day. I slept with it going. It was awful because it was so awkward and cumbersome, but it was necessary. In the old days, like a couple years before, you were put in a cast and three months later, you came out of it with an atrophied leg that could not bend. With the CPM machine, the bones healed without any pressure being placed on them while the joint moved, keeping my muscles working.

My leg hurt every time it bent to its maximum limit. It was excruciating at the beginning and I had to take painkillers. I didn't want to take them, but I found myself begging for them. If the nurse was one minute late in bringing them to me, I'd say, "Excuse me, where are the painkillers?" As an athlete, I would take aspirin when I was injured because it's an anti-inflammatory. I also took prescription drugs when a doctor said I needed them. But this was pain at its worst.

When I could, I looked at my leg. It was just so ugly: stitches everywhere, a bump filled with scar tissue, and a six-inch, half-moon scar that will last forever. I announced I was never wearing a skirt again. I hadn't yet thought about tennis clothes.

My stomach and hip area were killing me too. A cough or a laugh sent me through the roof because of the bone-graft surgery. The doctors had cut into me as if I were having a cesarean section. One of those first days after the surgery, a physical therapist and a nurse came in to prop me up and teach me how to stand. First, the nurse wanted me to sit up and reach for a triangle they had dangling in front of me. She propped me up and I reached out for it, but it was so painful, I leaned back again. I thought she would be there to hold me up, but she wasn't behind me, so I fell back into the bed, screaming. I had no control over my stomach muscles and ripped every single one. What more could I do to myself?

I was in the hospital for about a week, until I could maneuver on crutches on my own. The only thing that made the stay tolerable was the daily visits from family and friends. There were ten people in my room every night. My father always ordered pizza or Mexican food for the group. Then I went home—and I mean home, to my parents' house. I needed twenty-four-hour care.

I had therapy to go to, but otherwise, I simply sat in the backyard with my three dogs at my feet, a small table with the telephone by my side, and my diary and several books in my lap. That was how I lived my days. I went to therapy Mondays, Wednesdays, and Fridays. Otherwise, I was just hanging out.

I think now that the most peaceful months of my life were those after the accident. I quickly accepted that there was nothing I could do about it. I realized how lucky I was to be alive, and I knew my only obligation was to learn how to walk again. There I was, goal-oriented Tracy Austin, hoping to walk.

One of my diary entries was dated Tuesday, August 22, 1989, 4 P.M., parents' backyard:

I feel very at peace with myself and life. Things seem

brighter and more vivid. Smells are more aromatic. There is not much I can do about my situation, so I might as well do the best I can. I've been reading *Shogun,* and *Living, Loving and Learning* by Leo Buscaglia. He really points out how wonderful life is and you really choose to decide how full and exciting your life is. I think I feel so at peace because I realize how frail and fragile life is. I could have been history very easily in the accident. I feel so blessed to have been allowed to come out of this treacherous accident with only a broken knee. I feel happy and vibrant and full of life. I find myself less tense, noticing the beautiful things in the world more, and smelling the roses. I notice all the gorgeous flowers and wonders of nature.

Why am I so happy when it seems like I've had one injury after another, and then this? I am surprised myself, but I am content because I have already led such a full and interesting life up to age 26. The exciting experiences I've had most will never be lucky to feel. And maybe I would have won more titles, but I don't see too many people at the top real happy. Most of them look like they have a whole side of themselves missing from life. I'd rather have this inner peace than all the titles.

I was unbelievably unlucky to have had the accident, but to survive being hit by a man going sixty miles per hour was incredibly lucky. If he had been a split-second slower, he would have hit my door and I would have been killed. One more second and he could have missed me. But at least he hit the strongest part of my car, the wheel base.

Funny, I never heard from him, but my lawyers are talking to his lawyers.

I had the surgery on my knee on August 7 and went home on August 14. I started therapy on August 17. For a year, I would go to Centinela to work with my therapist, Clive Brewster. Therapy was boring. In the first three months, I went for one hour a day, three days a week. In the fourth month, I moved up to two to three hours a day, five days a week. It wasn't like I was building huge muscles and had daily progress. It was tedious, tedious work. The first thing I would do when I got there was tighten my quadriceps (thigh), ten seconds on, ten seconds off. Then I'd move to heel digs, ten seconds on, ten seconds off.

The very first day of therapy, I couldn't tighten my thigh muscle. Couldn't even flex it. It just sat there. It took me one to two weeks to get a twitch. "My God," I said, "I have a long way to go."

Eventually, I would get on the stationary bike and either push up on the pedal, or push down. But not both. If I went around, I would bend my knee too much.

The CPM machine was taking care of moving my knee. It would bend it thirty degrees, then fifty-five degrees, and finally, ninety degrees. When I moved to a new degree setting, it was grueling. My knee wouldn't move. I was creaking like the Tin Man. Clive didn't damage anything by forcing it to move more; he just was pushing to get the most out of my knee. Degrees became a way to measure my progress. I got my full range of motion back before December, when I still was on crutches.

I didn't sleep very well with the CPM machine hooked up. I'd say I tossed and turned, but I couldn't even do that because my leg was attached to the machine. For weeks, I had to use a bedpan. Then, when I could get up to go to the bathroom in the middle of the night, I had to ring a bell beside my bed to wake up my mother. She came in and helped me put my leg into the removable cast, then pushed me up, and got me on my crutches. This is the way I got up every single morning, too. I was an invalid. In the bathtub, my right leg would sit in the water, unable to move. After helping me out of the tub and into my clothes, my mother got me my breakfast. I couldn't even carry a plate because of my crutches. She took my breakfast outside and got me all set to eat and read and talk on the phone. She left for an hour or two to play tennis, then came back to pick me up and take me to therapy, then take me home again.

She and my dad, who drove me when my mother couldn't, were saints. They did everything for me. I never, ever could have recovered alone. Of course, they were there with me when I was a child, but they were also there again when I became an adult and needed them even more. Isn't that a nice thing to be able to say?

I started walking again in early December. My routine at therapy was that I would take my crutches over to the weight machine, get on the machine, and start to do my exercises. When I moved to one crutch, I would lean on that until the last moment, then sit down.

One day, Clive watched me get into position, then took away my crutch.

I thought he was teasing until I got off the machine and wanted to move to another. "I can't do it," I said.

"Yes, you can."

I slowly put my right leg down. I gained my balance and moved carefully. Tears streamed down my face, tears of joy. I was walking again. In my diary that day, I wrote that "I was scared and exhilarated at the same time. I started to cry, so I walked faster so no one would see me."

It dawned on me that Clive was just like Robert Lansdorp, pushing me to do something I didn't think I could do.

I wrote in my diary what it felt like to stand on my leg. "It feels like my body is so heavy I won't be able to stand up. It's like somebody is putting a couch on my head and I have to try to stand on one leg."

There were little victories, but they were followed by long periods of absolutely nothing but work. The doctors and Clive told me it would take twelve months to get back to being a normal person—not an athlete, an ordinary person—and it took twelve months.

For some reason, I turned the pressure down on myself during that year. I couldn't be focused anymore, with six, seven months to go. I would have been a basket case. If something good happened, I wouldn't let myself get too excited, because if you're excited at the beginning, you get too disappointed during the lulls. I gave myself time. I didn't worry if I couldn't do something one day because I knew I had so many months to go, it didn't matter. I can't believe I was this patient. I guess athletes learn to deal with injuries because they are such a part of our lives.

I wasn't particularly eager to hit a tennis ball, but one day in the early fall, Cecelia Fernandez helped me onto a court at the Kramer Club, put me in a small deck chair, and hit the ball directly to me. I sat there and hit volleys. We laughed; I felt so awkward, sitting down and hitting a tennis ball. But I enjoyed being around the sport again. I sometimes would go with my mom to the Kramer Club and hang out there, reading a book while she played. I enjoyed that. Surprisingly, it didn't make me angry to be around people who could play.

In late September, my mother, my sister Pam, Pam's friend Robin, my old-boyfriend-turned-good-friend Greg, and I went to the Volvo men's tournament at UCLA. We go every year. It's a family ritual. I had my wheelchair in the car for long stretches like shopping, but, otherwise, I hobbled in on crutches. The wheelchair made me feel funny. I hated being taken care of that much, especially in front of a crowd. I'm sure most people knew who I was. I was embarrassed, but I slowly worked my way to my seat and propped my leg across Greg's lap.

The announcer called out my name and had me wave from my seat. Johnny Carson was there that night, too, and he also was introduced to the crowd.

As I was watching the beginning of one of the matches, my eye caught a handsome man walking up the stairs. I wanted to make eye contact with him, but when he looked at me, I looked straight at the ground. Twenty-six years old and I still was incredibly shy. So much for us.

Between matches, Robin, my sister Pam's crazy friend, stood up.

"Seen any good-looking guys around here?" she said to me.

"There's one, right there," I said. I pointed toward him. He was only ten feet away.

"I'll be right back," Robin said.

"Robin, no, are you crazy?" I said. But she was gone.

She walked right over to the guy and said, without even introducing herself, "What do you do for a living?"

Thinking she was off the wall, he joked, "I'm a taxidermist. Why do you want to know?"

"My friend wants to meet you."

Robin brought him over and said, "Tracy, this is a friend of mine. I'd like you to meet Scott."

Scott Holt is not a taxidermist. He used to teach tennis during the summer in college and now is in mortgage banking. But he sat down anyway, between my mom and me, and joined us for the rest of the evening. He had a buddy there who was very talkative, but Scott said next to nothing. I found out later he was confused because he thought Greg was my boyfriend. I guess having my leg draped over him had something to do with the misconception.

As we said good-bye, he didn't ask for my phone number. But I found out later he had asked Robin for my number, and thinking she should be protective, she wouldn't give it to him and got his number for me.

I told myself to forget about him because my love life was in transition. I was leaving town to visit my boyfriend Wolf Mack at Carnegie-Mellon in Pittsburgh, where he was attending graduate school. We were going to end our relationship. In the same week my accident occurred, he was getting ready to start graduate school. Our priorities took very dramatic and opposite turns. He was going to be busy with classes and studying fourteen hours a day. And I was going to have fourteen free hours a day.

I had met Wolf the year before, when I stayed with his family in Franklin Lakes, New Jersey, while playing doubles at Mahwah with Stephanie Rehe during the beginning of my comeback. We reached the semis, which wasn't bad. I was playing a lot of doubles because I figured that would get me ready for singles.

Anna Maria Fernandez was staying at the Macks' house the week of Mahwah, as she had for years. I wanted to stay with a family because that always was more fun than staying in a hotel by myself. She said the Macks were great, so I asked the people in charge of housing to let me stay with them, and they did.

"Their son is really cute," Anna Maria told me. "So don't come home like you usually do after practice. Clean up a little."

When I think of Wolf, I think of New York City and my comeback. The idea to come back began at the White House in 1987, when I played an exhibition with Jimmy Arias. He said he was surprised at how well I was playing and that I had to play again. I listened to him.

In the beginning of 1988, I practiced with Kathrin Keil, a player on the circuit. I hurt my foot and was out for a while, then came back in San Diego in July 1988, playing doubles with Robin White. We lost in the first round, but that was OK. I was just so incredibly happy to be playing again after almost five years off the circuit. On my way to the tournament, I was singing madly to Diana Ross's "I'm Coming Out." I was so excited to be playing again. After the match, I said I was having the time of my life.

For so many years, people had said I was burned out, or asked if and when I was going to play again. Well, this answered those questions. Playing again was all I had wanted to do for the last five years—and now I finally was doing it.

I realized, however, that when I first started, my nerves were not OK. I was a wreck. This was going to take a while. I didn't know how to concentrate anymore. I didn't feel normal right away.

I went on to play mixed doubles with Ken Flach at the 1988 Open. We lost in the semifinals to Liz Smiley and Patrick McEnroe and we lost bad—1 and 0. After the match, I found out Ken tanked it.

He and his men's doubles partner, Robert Seguso, had a Reebok commercial to shoot when the mixed doubles final was scheduled. "That won't be a problem," Robert said so enough people heard it.

Sure enough, it wasn't. I had never played with anyone who threw a match before, so it took me a set and a half to realize what was happening. Ken had not won his serve to that point and was playing in the alley, leaving me to cover three fourths of the court. I finally realized and I couldn't believe it. It was an important match for me and he didn't even care.

I played women's doubles with Mary Joe Fernandez and reached the third round—again, a decent showing. I played a couple more doubles matches that year, getting to the semis a few times, and I was heartened. I knew I could do it. Physically, I was getting closer. It was the mental part I really needed to work on.

At the beginning of 1989, I played a couple exhibitions and one had a familiar ending. I defaulted with a pulled hip flexor.

I finally moved into singles at the Virginia Slims event in Palm Springs in March. I played Nicole Provis and lost in three sets, 7–5, 5–7, 6–1. I was playing myself into shape, but my problem was concentration. I was exhausted from being so nervous. I felt the eyes of every reporter and every coach and every player and every fan on me. Tracy Austin, on the comeback trail. It was tough. I was thinking too much, no longer the child who just went out and played. It would have been nice if my name at that moment could have been changed to Sue Smith.

I remember Robert sitting in the stands in Palm Springs. In the third set, he yelled, "Come on, fight!"

I smiled and said, "I'm trying, but I'm so tired, I can't even think."

I talked to Pancho Gonzalez, a former world champion, and he said it took him a full year before he felt comfortable again—and he had been away only two years.

All the while, I was dating Wolf. At times it was long distance, but I tried to be in New York City, where he lived, as much as possible. (It was later that he went to Carnegie-Mellon in Pittsburgh.) He was a chemical engineer, lived on Seventy-fifth and Riverside Drive, and pretty soon, when I wasn't at a tournament, I was living there, too. It was so different for me, and so much fun. I became a commuter, walking to the subway, taking the subway to the train, then a cab to the tennis academy at Port Washington to practice and train. At night, Wolf and I would go to the Korean deli around the corner and walk home to fix dinner. We went to museums, book stores, and art openings. I became a New Yorker. How strange, and how interesting. Another new thing for me.

I shared the apartment with Wolf and his two roommates. All of us shared one bathroom. That was, well, gross. Three guys and me. Enough said.

When I had to do an appearance in Japan for a week, Wolf came with me. I admired how adventurous he was, trying everything and taking the train all over the country by himself.

After Palm Springs, I played some more doubles and hurt my foot. In the summer I decided I was well enough to play team tennis with the New Jersey Stars to be near Wolf. Then came the accident.

Wolf came to the hospital Thursday when he heard the news and again on Friday and told me he would come again on Saturday morning at about nine o'clock.

He didn't show up, so I called him. Because I was leaving Sunday, this would be the last day I was going to see him for a while. I was miserable and I needed him. I found him at his parents' home in New Jersey, eating pancakes with his family on the deck. How wonderful, I thought.

He said he would come at eleven. When he didn't show up then, I called again. He was out in the lake swimming with his father. That saved me the trouble of telling him where to jump.

I met Scott at the tournament a few weeks later. I figured I never would see him again, but he didn't forget about me. He again asked Robin for my number, but she wouldn't give it out. He remembered where Pam worked and called her to ask for my number, but she wouldn't give it out.

Pam told me and I told her to call Scott back and give him my number. Finally, she did. The poor guy. When he finally got hold of me, he thought I wasn't interested in him.

Finally, on October 3, on crutches, I had my first date with Scott Holt. I told him I admired his persistence. As of spring 1992, I'm still dating Scott. He's perfect for me because he's so different from me. For instance, he's very laid back. If we were both like me, one of us would have killed the other by now. He has a wonderful sense of humor and gets a kick out of all kinds of people. I have to pull him away from conversations with everyone, even the clerk at the yogurt store.

Our first date was funny because we ran into Jim Pugh, my old tennis exhibition opponent, at the restaurant. We saw him as we were leaving at about ten-thirty in the evening. The next morning, I went to the Nancy Reagan tennis tournament at ten o'clock. I took Greg with me, again as a friend. And who do I see but Jim Pugh.

"I saw you with one guy who has brown hair and now you're with this guy with blond hair," he said. "It's been only twelve hours."

On my third date with Scott, we stayed at the beach talking until all hours. When we decided to leave, his car wouldn't start. He had put the heat on as we talked and then the car didn't work. He walked across the street and knocked on the door of a guy who had his TV on—we could see the light through the windows—and he called AAA.

By the time I got home to my parents' house, it was six in the morning. I told my mom the car wouldn't start.

"In my day, we used to say we ran out of gas," she said with a smile.

As I went to therapy and got better, I tried to lead as normal a life as possible. I bought the brand-new, five-bedroom home I live in now on a hill in Redondo Beach, a couple blocks from the Pacific Ocean. (The most-asked question: Do you have a tennis court? No. I barely have a yard in front or back, but the patio, gardens, and ocean view more than make up for it.)

I moved in on December 15, 1989, when I was well enough to be on my own again. My life was two things: decorating and rehabilitating. Buying furniture, pillows, and knick-knacks became a delight and a diversion. I bought dozens of plants and flowers. My mom came over and helped me get started with the gardening.

That year in New York had been my farthest from my home and family. The accident took me back to them, to the garden in the backyard, to be taken care of. My mom said that was probably the only good thing about the accident, that she got to see me again. I made sure that didn't change when I moved into my new house.

At about the same time I moved, I got in a car and drove again. I was very scared to do it; I took service roads all the way to therapy. I found myself doing something that day that I now do all the time: I slowed down as I neared intersections, even when the light was green as could be. I looked both ways, then went across.

In April at Hilton Head, I finally hit a tennis ball while standing up. I still couldn't run; I just had to stand there and hit. Eight months after the accident, I could stand still and hit a ball. A little victory.

I still was in rehabilitation and sometimes the people undergoing therapy got to me. One guy there had a broken ankle and he was whining and complaining after only one week. I had been there ten months at that point. The poor guy was loony tunes because he couldn't jog. Boy, did he have a long way to go.

It was a year after the accident, August 1990, before I could be myself, running, planting my feet, moving around on the tennis court. I was back to being a healthy person, but I was not back to being an athlete. That part started to happen when I began working with Ken Matsuda, my trainer, after I got back from the 1990 U.S. Open, where I worked for USA Network. Ken, who worked with Michael Chang, has pushed me to the point where now I am about halfway along the road from being a healthy person to being a competitive professional athlete. Whether I can go the rest of the way, I don't know. We'll see if my knee can take it.

Although it now is several years behind me, I still think of the accident and the way it changed my life. Every now and then, I see something that triggers a thought that gets me upset. Around Christmas one year, Scott rented a movie, *Dead Calm,* which has a dreadful car accident scene in which a baby flies through the window. I started to cry.

Not long ago, I went to the opening ceremony of the California Special Olympics. There were thousands of kids there, all mentally disabled in some way. The children didn't even realize it; they were so happy. They love the simple things in life. They gave the Pledge of Allegiance in such beautiful voices that day. I followed them by reciting the Special Olympian's pledge.

Then a man who was paralyzed in a car accident seven years ago came onto the field and sang a song, and that really moved me. They had to install a special ramp just to get him out on the field. I was sitting at the top of the stands with my friends. I had just walked up there. That man could never do that. And the same thing happened to both of us; we were victims of car accidents.

I am so lucky. Yes, I lost a year of my life. But I can walk.

# CHAPTER EIGHT

When you look at what is going on right now in women's tennis, I ask one favor: Don't blame me.

I know, I know. I was the first young girl to take over women's tennis. Now, teenagers basically own the game. It began innocently, but I guess I sure started something. I imagine some of these girls chart their progress by the precedents I set. If a little girl is fourteen now and not playing in the pros and winning the U.S. Open at sixteen, she and/or her parents must think she is way behind. I get fathers who shall remain nameless, telling me they view today's top players as their daughters' rivals—and their daughters are twelve years old.

This is lunacy. This isn't the natural progression of a child into a sport, which happily was exactly the experience I had. My parents never, ever pushed.

No, a lot of times this is parental pressure. And it's all about dollar signs.

I did television commentary at the Forum in Los Angeles not long ago and met the father of an up-and-coming new phenomenon. I asked the father how his children became involved in tennis. He very honestly told me he decided his kids would be tennis players when he watched someone receive a runner-up check for thirty thousand dollars at a tournament. This is before the children were conceived. He decided that when he and his wife had kids, they would become tennis players. I don't mean to pick on him, because he has good intentions and wants the best for his family, but I worry about the consequences of action like that.

My brother Jeff always claims I was the start of it because I accomplished a lot so young. But I really wasn't the beginning of this. For me, becoming a professional was both naive and natural. I just fell into that tournament in Portland. I didn't want to turn pro. I kept going to school. These days, by the time kids are eight, they know they are going to play on the circuit. Someday, I would love to see a story on tennis camps—not on the kids who make it, but on the hundreds who give up their youth and leave their homes and families, all for tennis, and don't succeed. Most children are not born to be tennis champions, yet it seems as if parents don't understand that. We may be hurting more children than we are helping in these tennis camps. I don't know. But I worry about it.

Misconceptions develop about any public figure, so I accept the fact that every now and then, people will get something wrong about me. But what really irritates me is that almost everyone believes I was pushed into tennis by oppressive parents, and now today's parents are using them as an excuse to pressure their own kids because they think it works.

My mother and father never, ever pushed me. One of the first to get a bad reputation on the circuit for being a pushy parent was Andrea Jaeger's father. I often watched him be tough on Andrea and felt sorry for her, but I also believe Andrea had to want what she was going after or else she wouldn't have gotten that far. You don't get to the top rung of women's tennis without having your own drive and discipline.

My mom never yelled. She watched my lessons, yes, but she was working at the club, too. When I began playing in the pros, she sent me off on my own only once, to Houston, where I couldn't take care of myself—and have the room-service bill to prove it. She went with me the next week to Minneapolis, and never left me unaccompanied again. It was so nice to have a friend with me on the road. I loved the support she provided for me. As for my father, he probably is the least pushy person in the world. He would have loved to have five rocket scientists in the family. To both of them, tennis is one thing: a game.

In fact, my parents and I floundered because we were not aggressive enough. When I was injured, we never found the right doctor. I can't see a Stefano Capriati doing that, just sitting back and watching a career end. But I've got to hand it to Peter Graf. He called probably every thumb specialist in the world when Steffi had her skiing accident.

Consider the times. It has been less than a decade since I left tennis, but it might as well be another century. The game has become such a business. The women make more than ten times the thirty-nine thousand dollars I made for winning the U.S. Open in 1979, and endorsements have gone through the roof. And to think I was probably making more money than anyone when I was playing, with the possible exception of Chris.

Furthermore, the players look like race car drivers with all the patches they wear. I wanted to wear a Ted Tinling dress that I paid for because it was prestigious and beautiful. Put a patch on that? No way.

Then again, I have my own clothes line now, so if I were playing on the circuit, I'd wear that. And I'd probably put a patch on, too. If I got paid a hundred thousand dollars to wear, say, FORD on my arm, I'd do it.

The stakes are higher. So is every tennis parents' blood pressure.

There are two types of parents in the game. The first kind are the ones who sacrifice for the kid, who give up their jobs and move with the child and hope that he or she eventually becomes good enough to pay everyone's living expenses. The second type are the Austins and the Everts, among others. With my family, or Chris's, there was some sense of normalcy. I didn't build the family a two-million-dollar house. Chris didn't do that, either. Our fathers kept their jobs and missed quite a few tournaments because they had to work.

My mom, for instance, graduated from UCLA, then got married. My dad is a physicist. They had lives of their own and children to raise and groceries to buy. But my mom did get to spend more time with me traveling on the circuit because the other four already had grown up.

Basically, the distinction comes down to this: The first kind of tennis family puts tremendous pressure on the child to support them financially, while the second kind allows the child to do nice things for the family in terms of gifts, while keeping the pressure off.

Way back in 1978, my parents talked to Barry Lorge, then of *The Washington Post,* about parental pressure and the way they brought me up. My father said:

> There is a more subtle pressure. That is when the parents are simply too interested. Not harsh, but so interested that the child feels a burden. If Tracy gets a little testy about us being too involved, we back off a little bit. We can sense how she feels day to day, and act accordingly. We don't want to swarm all over her. Some parents are at every practice. My wife watches Tracy's lessons, so she can help her understand what she's supposed to learn, but she doesn't hover around, dwelling on every shot.

And my mother said in the same interview:

> She's become more independent, but she still has a hard time making up her mind about anything. She's caught in between wanting to be led like a child and to be allowed to make her own decisions like an adult. She's

in that transition period, so we sometimes have to map out her day for her.

But we're careful not to put too much pressure on her. We try to motivate her when she's down and be supportive.

Too many times it's the parents who want their child to be a champion, and that doesn't work. The child himself has to want it, to have the desire and the discipline to make the necessary sacrifices. I don't think you can want anything for someone else.

I read an article that said Jennifer's father changed coaches when she was ten because the new coach taught a great serve. I was switching around a bit from age sixteen on. But ten? That's almost like planning a corporation. Mr. Capriati has done a great job—Jennifer's game is very complete. It's just a different philosophy now. It doesn't happen naturally anymore. It's planned for a long time. There are different coaches for different parts of the game: serve, running, conditioning. A lot of times, it's assembly-line tennis.

But it's not all the fathers' fault. In juniors, I never had agents come up and talk to me at tournaments. Now, when a good player is ten, agents and endorsement people are around all the time. Jennifer had deals worth a guaranteed five million dollars—spread out over several years—before she played her first match.

Not long ago, I saw a TV report on a ten-year-old Los Angeles player. She was asked what single thing she wanted from tennis.

"To get rich," she said.

For the longest time, I was the symbol for the youth movement in tennis in the United States. But I have been supplanted, finally and thankfully, by Jennifer. I like her and think she is an excellent player. So much has happened to her so fast, yet she remains a good kid both on and off the court. She has handled herself with poise and concentration on the court, with giggles and shy grins off it. Who doesn't like that?

Now, she has become the measure for young tennis stars. The day she signed for five million dollars, I'll bet five million parents pushed their kids into tennis.

So much has been made of Jennifer Capriati that if she doesn't become Number One, some people might be disappointed. The build-up has been that big. There was no lead time for her, no chance to get to know her. Just, *boom,* Jennifer. It's almost unfair that she didn't have a chance to get her feet wet without all of us watching. With all this press and attention, if she is not one of the greatest players of all time, people are going to be very disappointed. But I think she has lived up to expectations very well.

Fans have really taken to her. Chris Evert was doing TV commentary at Hilton Head and Scott Holt, who was there with me, watched people run after Jennifer for her autograph.

Then he saw them come back to Chris and say, "Oh, and you, too."

Unbelievable.

Then there's Monica Seles. Monica has been quoted as saying she will get out of the game at age twenty-five, when her budding acting career takes over, and she hopes to win her first Academy Award soon after. Despite her intrigue and controversy, Monica is good for the game. At seventeen, she handles the pressure and media attention very well. She usually is pretty accommodating and open about what she says. She talks nonstop and is quite thoughtful for a teenager.

I was working at the 1991 Wimbledon for NBC when Monica mysteriously pulled out. She said she had shin splints, but it took quite a while to get that answer. It's the biggest tournament in the world and she was the Number One seed. She is getting more than a million dollars a year from the tour and when officials and sponsors asked why she was pulling out, she owed them an answer. You have to have a reason. I heard that Women's Tennis Association executive director Gerald Smith called her many times a day, and her agent Stephanie

Tolleson wouldn't say anything either. Monica and Stephanie had more of a responsibility when she pulled out at the last minute like that. Wimbledon and the sports world deserved a better answer. I don't think she realized it was going to become that big a deal, but she really learned from the experience.

Communication can be a problem. When I was working for *Good Morning America* at Wimbledon, Steffi won the tournament and we wanted to have her on. I didn't have her number, so I went to the WTA office at the tournament and figured they could give me the number or get her for me. That's the way it worked when I was playing.

Well, things have changed. I was informed that Georgina Clark, a WTA tour official, was the only one allowed to call Steffi. And she didn't want to bother her. I couldn't believe it. I had to beg her to call and ask her. It was like I was asking for the Queen of England.

Georgina finally got on the phone and began asking Steffi how her dogs were and what she was doing—just shooting the breeze. I was in the room with Georgina and nearly died. I mouthed the words: "Just ask her!" Finally, she did and Steffi said she'd do it, of course, and gave a great interview.

Back when I was playing, the WTA would call and say, "Tracy, can you do it?" and I'd say sure and do it. No one was afraid to ask. Now they treat the players with kid gloves. It's amazing how even agents and tour officials are afraid of their own players.

As a player and a television commentator, I have found several things in our sport that confound me. That's one. Another is the on-court behavior of players. John McEnroe questions line calls frequently during his matches. I think he does it because he has such a competitive nature and wants to win so badly, he can't control himself. John also is quite sensitive; I was eating breakfast at an exhibition in Mexico and he came along and sat down with me. For the next two hours, he opened up, telling me about his concerns and his worries about his career. I was pleasantly surprised to see the depth of his feelings and his many insights about his life.

As for the fits and tantrums, most of the time, they only hurt and undermine the players themselves. There are very few people who can throw a fit and not have it negatively affect them. I can think of three names: Jimmy Connors, John McEnroe, and Ilie Nastase. With them, their opponent has a tough time dealing with it. It seems like they do it to get themselves going and the opponent gets thrown off by it.

Jimmy Connors's play at the 1991 U.S. Open was something else again. It was terrific Jimmy made it to the semis. As a thirty-nine-year-old, he gave us all hope. I love his enthusiasm for the game of tennis and the sheer joy he seems to get from playing it. I admire Jimmy's intensity and ability to stay focused over the last twenty years, and I love to watch him play more than anyone, but I sometimes wish he could curtail the derogatory remarks he occasionally makes on the court.

Players are getting away with too much these days. I saw a player spit at an umpire without getting a warning. The umpire just let him get away with it. If Michael Jordan did that to a referee, he would get a technical. In fact, he did this year—and got kicked out of the game. Other sports would have officials throw someone out of the game. But not tennis.

Nonetheless, it's a great time for women's tennis. Steffi Graf's domination has been ended by the emergence of Monica Seles, Gabriela Sabatini, and Jennifer Capriati, and the staying power of Martina Navratilova.

I don't know Steffi very well. In some ways, I feel sorry for her. It's kind of stupid to feel sorry for her, but she seems unhappy sometimes and doesn't appear to know who to turn to for advice. Her father, who has been the subject of a couple of nasty rumors, has brought her a lot of anxiety. It's almost like there's not a safe haven for her anymore. It's a competitive life especially because she's been Number One for so long and her opponents are gunning for her, and it's difficult to know where to turn for help and friendship.

At the U.S. Open in 1991, I saw Steffi joyfully playing with Mary Joe Fernandez's little niece in the locker room. It sounds silly to say this, but it was nice to see a side of Steffi I never had seen before.

But on the court, if Steffi's on, she usually will win. She has more athletic talent than the others. Her quickness is the key. She doesn't hit her backhand as well as her forehand, but an opponent can't pick on it because she's able to run around it and hit so many winners. Steffi relies on her serve, her huge forehand, and her quickness. She's got three great weapons. That's what you see in the top players, they've either got one aspect of their game that is outstanding, or several very, very good weapons. This is what makes them Numbers One, Two, and Three, rather than Number Twenty-five.

For instance, Mary Joe doesn't have one huge forte—not her serve, her forehand, her backhand, her volley—but she's so consistent and so mentally tough on the key points that she wins. She's just kind of there, but she doesn't miss, she doesn't give away free points, and rarely has a bad loss. She never tries for stupid shots. That's her weapon, consistency in tournaments.

Monica has a heart as big as the house she will own and simply never gives up. Her mental toughness is what I had. I wish she had been at Wimbledon in 1991 to try for the Grand Slam. Monica on grass would have been interesting.

Her game is great. She is lethal. Every single point, she is moving her opponent so deep and hitting so hard. She doesn't give up on any point and plays great on the big points. She comes at you, comes at you, comes at you. Mentally, she must be the strongest player out there right now. She also has an advantage being Number One. No matter what you tell yourself, if you are playing the top-ranked player in the world, you think about it. You lose some confidence. It has to happen. I was commentating on the 1991 Virginia Slims tournament in Los Angeles for Prime Ticket, a regional cable network, when Kimiko Date played Monica in the final. Kimiko went up 3–0 in the first set and was playing just beautifully, totally in control. All of a sudden, it was as if a button were pushed in her mind: "I'm playing the Number One person in the world." She stopped playing aggressively. Nothing worked—and Monica won easily.

I watched her play in March and she was ahead, 6–2, 4–0, and lost a point and got mad at herself. Everyone laughed—but I flashed back and remembered that's exactly how intense I was. I didn't want to lose one point. She also has plans for her career, just the way I did. At seventeen, most kids are trying to decide what college they want to go to. She knows what she wants from tennis—as well as from life.

Considering her lack of a support group compared to others, you have to give her a lot of credit that she does so well. She has no physical trainer and no official coach other than her father, yet she is killing everyone else.

You can see it in her eyes, in her concentration level. Most players let up at certain times, like when they get ahead, but she remains tough at the most difficult times.

And she turns what could be a handicap into another advantage. She hits both a two-handed backhand and a two-handed forehand. When a player uses two hands on both sides, she has to be closer to the ball to get it, which means her balance has to be better and she has to be faster, and her reach is cut down.

If you hit a one-handed shot, you can lunge for the ball and flick at it with your wrist. That's not the case hitting two-handed. But the advantage of two-handed shots is the strength and control they afford.

I saw Jennifer beat Monica in the final at San Diego in 1991 and I was certain my record of being the youngest U.S. Open winner was going to be broken by Jennifer. I had never seen a match where two women hit the ball that hard on every shot. I was amazed.

At the Open, I went into the locker room and saw them both as they prepared for their semifinal match. Jennifer was totally relaxed, getting her ankle taped and munching on a frozen orange juice cup. Monica was stoic and quiet, eating pasta. Before a match, I was more like Monica.

When they went onto the court and began playing, I couldn't believe the pace at which they hit the ball—and most of their shots went in. In the third set, Jennifer served for the match two times and I could see her let up and lose it. That's where she differs from a true champion; they apply more pressure when the match is tight. Monica won it because she is more experienced and tougher than Jennifer right now. But Jennifer still has plenty of time.

Gabriela Sabatini intrigues me. She has improved a lot. She used to have rather loopy strokes and used to hit the ball off her back foot, falling away from the ball, which is not technically correct. She used up a lot of extra energy, became tired, and had some trouble in the third set. Now, however, she is fresher and coming to the net more, hitting flat strokes with a more compact swing and stepping into the ball much better. That improvement and her new-found aggressiveness are what allowed her to win the 1990 U.S. Open.

Jennifer is terrific. After seeing her at Wimbledon in 1991, I now know how complete a player she is. Her serve—the actual service motion—is great. Her strokes are very sound technically. I love how compact they are. She hits the ball with her weight shifting to her front foot: just perfect. She is big and strong: five feet nine. That could become a problem for her because she could get too big. Nonetheless, she has the mind to play this game and she's got much better strokes than Steffi or Monica. She is much more technically sound and she's fast. She's not missing anything and there is so much room for her to grow. If I had a daughter and had to choose a style of play for her, I would pick Jennifer's.

Although Jennifer had a good year in 1991, it didn't seem to me that she did as well as she did in her first year, but that's where pressure and expectations come into play. There were no expectations the first year and now there are many. And I do think the pressure will get to her at some time or another. In fact, I think it happened after the Australian Open in 1992. She lost in the quarters there, then lost in the first round in a tournament in Japan. It was too much for her. She's been doing a lot of exhibitions. It's a tough life. To me, it looks as if she isn't having as much fun out there as she was before. It's beginning to look as if it's a job for her.

Another matter people bring up is school. Some question how these kids miss eight weeks at the end of the school year due to the French Open and preparation for Wimbledon and still lead a seminormal school life. I couldn't do it so I skipped the French, but if they can, I've got to hand it to them. (For that matter, I didn't play the French or the Australian until I had graduated from high school.) Who knows what the other kids are doing, but I have a lot of respect for Mary Joe. She stayed in regular school, got straight A's and was there at her graduation.

I've watched the current stars enough to know their strengths and weaknesses, but I know the women I played with and against even better. I am big on technique, just hitting through the line of the ball. That's what I did so well in my career and why I hit the ball so hard and so pure.

I had to use my body weight and have proper balance because I was so small. Many players don't do that. I was always amazed by McEnroe. He is such a great athlete with so much talent that he can get away with pulling up on the ball when he hits it. We're all told to bend our knees low on volleys, but his hands are so good, he doesn't always need to. With these new, oversize racquets, John will be the last of the great finesse players. His slices, his touch shots, the way his racquet caresses the ball—this will leave tennis when he does. Everyone is into power now.

Of all the players I competed against, Hana Mandlikova had the most talent. When she got up to an easy forehand, she could do twenty things with it. I had three choices, so it wasn't as difficult. I just hit the ball and won the point. Hana, however, might have tried an underspin drop shot angle—a very low percentage shot. All the options get confusing. Hana hits a lot of risky shots that make her fun to watch, though.

Martina is the other factor in the rankings today, just as she was ten years ago. That, by itself, is amazing. I think it's incredible she has had the motivation to stay focused for that long. It has been fun to see her gradually improve and add to her game. But when you play for that length of time, you are bound to have moments you'd rather forget, and I witnessed one at Wimbledon in 1991.

Martina was not herself over there, an emotional wreck in the wake of Judy Nelson's palimony lawsuit against her. You could tell her mind was on other things in her loss to Jennifer; it was really painful to watch. She was falling apart on Centre Court.

When I got home to California, I called her in Dallas and said if there was anything I could do, please to call. She'd been good to me and she looked so unhappy out on the court—and in so much pain, from her match and her life. Sometimes people think athletes are bigger than life and don't need support, but they do. She was so nice on the phone that day, and I was glad I called. She ended by saying, "I better run. My lawyers are coming in ten minutes."

We both laughed.

You see those big muscles on Martina but she really is quite sensitive. And unassuming—she'll talk to anybody. I've seen her chat with a man standing in line for an ice cream bar. Martina is probably the most superb female athlete of our generation. When I first came on the circuit, her backhand was a glaring weakness. She only could slice it without generating much power. But she worked hard on it and now has a topspin backhand that is much more of a weapon. She also had quite a temper in the late 1970s and early 1980s and was weaker emotionally. If it was 4–4 in the third set, I could break her down. Now, she doesn't crack.

Chris Evert never, ever, gave you anything. Her shot selection was very basic—either to hit it crosscourt or down the line, deep or with sharp angles. High-percentage, well-thought-out shots. I obviously was the same as Chris, having fewer choices. Some people might call that boring. I call it smart.

Once in a while when you played Martina, she would give you a free point, not on purpose, but just because of errors. Chris would never do that, nor would I, nor does Monica, it seems to me. That's why Monica will win so often.

All the young players now will last longer than I did because none of them will break down as I did. They can look at my downfall and say, "I won't do that. I'll train, I'll use weights. I won't make the mistakes Tracy made." In my defense, I'll say that I was the first, I had no role model. I also was only five feet four.

Some of today's players have trainers traveling with them. Training is such an integral part of their lives. It makes me sad, because if I had had that, I would have lasted so much longer. Of course, when you have millions and millions of dollars, you can afford to hire a support team.

Speaking of which, the money is so outrageous these days. All the players are so business-oriented. When I won the U.S. Open at sixteen, I didn't have a racquet contract because my agent and Wilson still were negotiating a deal. I got one the next year with Spalding. I didn't have a clothing contract because I didn't want a clothing contract. I got one later with Gunze. When I was young, I wanted to wear Ted Tinling's dresses.

Back when I won the 18 nationals, I was thrilled because the prize was a jacket made by Ted. When he told me he wanted to make a couple dresses for me, I couldn't have been prouder. He was such a part of tennis history. A few months after he died in 1990, I received a letter from the executor of his will. He told me Ted had left something for me: his pearl earring. I now have it in a box in my office at home. I was surprised and delighted he thought of me, as I was honored to wear his dresses. In fact, the last time I saw Ted, he reminded me, as he had for years, that the most important dress he was going to make for me was my wedding dress.

Money just wasn't as important to me when I was playing as it may be today. I was asked to do an ad for a tea company in Japan, but I said no because I didn't drink tea. Sara Kleppinger Forniciari suggested I go ahead and do it anyway. We laughed about it. No one was going to see it in the United States, but I still stuck to my guns and said no. Martina ended up doing it.

The next year, I was back in Japan, traveling with Sara, and it was freezing cold outside, so I ordered tea. Sara nearly fell off her chair. "Why didn't you like tea last year?" she asked me.

Even the length of Andre Agassi's hair is a financial decision. Nick Bollitieri said Andre won't cut his hair because it's worth five million dollars for all the publicity, notoriety, and resulting endorsements it brings him. He's very unusual and fans like unique people.

And when you see a neon Ray • Ban hat on a coach in the stands, that, too, is a business decision. Anyone in the player's entourage can be offered five hundred dollars to wear the hats as a promotion for the company. Even the former Soviet coaches wore the hats and collected the money.

At the U.S. Open in 1991, Aaron Krickstein's mother was in the stands, watching her son play Jimmy Connors. She looked great, as if she had just walked out of a beauty salon. This is one classy, well-to-do woman. But there was that Ray • Ban hat, propped on her hair.

A compelling issue that surrounds women in tennis—and women in almost all sports—is homosexuality. It's too bad that the public cares so much about it, because it really shouldn't matter. But the fact is it does seem to matter to people. I hope there will be a time when it will be acceptable for women to play sports without ever being thought of as masculine, but I don't think we're entirely there yet.

Why couldn't women perspire? Why did I, at age sixteen, feel

I had to hide the fact I was lifting weights at Laurie Belger's house? Why was there such a stigma about women as athletes? Thank goodness attitudes have changed, at least a little.

I can understand why some women on our circuit end up being attracted to other women. They get lonely on the road, and begin to gravitate to their peers on tour for emotional support. There are a lot of players who are married, and I have Scott. It's a very unusual man who has an ego that is strong enough to deal with a wealthy, famous woman athlete, yet who is sensitive enough to provide emotional support. They usually like to be the breadwinners and have their own careers. I still believe today that a girlfriend or wife traveling with a man on the circuit is not looked down upon as a man would be who is with a woman on the circuit. The man has to be confident enough not to worry about what people think of his untraditional role, which includes allowing the woman to have the spotlight. But he also has to be gentle enough to understand the bad times.

The women's tennis tour doesn't seem to have an image problem now. Monica, Jennifer, Gaby, and Steffi are attractive and feminine. Zina Garrison is married; Pam Shriver lets everyone know about her dates. Martina's life is well known because she is so honest. These are the high-profile players, the ones who make the difference in the marketing and promotion of the circuit. It's not like it was even five or ten years ago, when the palimony suit against Billie Jean forced her to lose all her endorsements.

# CHAPTER NINE

F rank Deford, the former *Sports Illustrated* writer, introduced me at a dinner at Pam Shriver's cystic fibrosis charity event in Baltimore in 1989. "The greatest rivalry in women's tennis was Chris and Martina," he said. "But maybe that wouldn't be the case if this woman had not gotten injured. Please welcome Tracy Austin."

If, if, if . . .

When I think about it, when I really let my mind wander, it makes me sad.

I'll be thirty on December 12, 1992. I have a wonderful existence, a beautiful home, a great man in my life, a close family, terrific friends, everything I could ever want. Except the sense that I fulfilled my potential on the tennis court.

Scott says I'm an enigma because people don't know where I've gone and what I'm doing. Some people think I'm barely scraping by and others think I'm making millions of dollars a year. Some think I'm delighted I don't have to play tennis anymore, while others think I'm depressed because I'm not playing. Most people at least know I'm alive, and a fair share still send me my two *Sports Illustrated* covers to auto-graph. My mom, who takes care of my fan mail, says she can tell when I've been on TV because the number of requests increases dramatically. Curry Kirkpatrick put my address in his story about me when I was thirteen, and my parents haven't moved, so it's easy for people to find me.

When people ask me what I do for a living, I tell them I am wearing about twelve hats and my life's as busy as ever. There most definitely is life beyond center court. I never have a typical day, which is what I like most about my life. I never want to sit still for long. I have become more spontaneous after my airport "kidnapping" by Bob Ruth. Yet I still have to plan out my days because I have so many commitments.

My life revolves around my travel schedule. I love to go on the road. I love to meet new people. And I feel completely comfortable in hotel rooms. I'm probably more relaxed there than at home, because the phone isn't constantly ringing and I can be alone to read or write. It's great because there are no household distractions.

I might be at home in Los Angeles Monday through Thursday, then I'll travel during the weekend. Here is an example: I gave a clinic at a charity tennis benefit in Washington, D.C., on a Friday night in September 1991, then flew to Chattanooga, Tennessee, on Saturday morning and worked all day as a spokeswoman for an athletic-shoe company, running a clinic and playing tennis with a hundred fifty inner-city children who were being exposed to tennis for the first time. I flew home Sunday.

Or, I might spend most of the week away and come home on the weekend. I participated in a charity pro-am for McDonald's in Wilmington, Delaware, in June 1991, playing dozens and dozens of games over two days with amateurs who paid a lot of money to play, and I also attended the required dinners and parties. What's fun about these events is when the people have fun. What's not fun is when they take it too seriously and think they are close to beating you. I end up doing quite a few of these in the East, so two days are required just for travel.

Other events require more time and are much more unique. The day before Thanksgiving in 1991, Jeff called and asked if I wanted to travel somewhere fun.

"No, I'm tired, I want to stay home," I said.

"How about Guam?" he asked.

"Where is Guam?"

"I don't know. I'll look at the globe."

Jeff found it and told me it was in the Pacific, which I faintly knew. Organizers were putting on a men's tennis tournament there and wanted to increase awareness of the sport by running some clinics for local children. That's what they wanted me to do.

I went for five days, had a great experience, and earned a fair amount of money for my work. I was there for my birthday, which was not forgotten. The school children sang "Happy Birthday" to me more times than I could count. What was really interesting was that it was such a key island in World War II and I loved learning the history of it. While Scott was scuba diving, he saw a lot of sunken boats and planes from the war.

In 1991, I participated in thirty-eight charity, corporate, and/or pro-am events. They ranged from corporate work for Virginia Slims to attending parties with Sudafed executives at the Women's Sports Foundation dinner in New York to running my own charity for the South Bay Children's Health Center. Charity work is vital; if I don't actually go and donate my time, I end up sending a racquet or autographed visor to be auctioned. I probably get twenty requests a month; my mom answers every one of them.

I also had eight different television assignments in 1991, including two weeks for NBC at Wimbledon, two weeks for USA Network at the U.S. Open, and a handful of individual telecasts for USA or Prime Ticket.

I don't like to talk about the specifics of my contracts, but all of this adds up to a very nice living. In addition, I still receive money from endorsements, some of which I've had since I was playing, others I've picked up since I left the circuit.

The biggest is my contract with Gunze. In 1978, I signed a deal with the company. They told Sara and Donald, my agents, that they like Americans and they like blondes. At first I wore Gunze tennis outfits in Japan. At every other tournament throughout the world, I wore Ted Tinling dresses. Then I signed with Spalding clothes, so I wore those clothes when I played everywhere but Japan.

Gunze finally said they wanted me in their clothes no matter where I played. They don't sell their clothes over here, but they didn't want pictures of me wearing any other clothes appearing in Japanese newspapers or on Japanese television.

Even now, I have my Gunze tennis wear line in Japan. I get catalogs from the company and have to laugh. There's TRACY AUSTIN on the front of a shirt in big letters, TRACY AUSTIN running down one of the legs of the pants in bigger letters, TRACY AUSTIN on the sleeve in even bigger letters. I have a roomful of these clothes, but, obviously, I can't wear them in the United States. I'm honored they want to use my name, but that can get a little embarrassing here at home.

I smile at the thought of Japanese people walking around with my name plastered all over their clothes. I also have to laugh at some of the promotional language in the catalog: "Come ride on orange wind with Tracy Austin." They take words they think sound nice together and make sentences with them. They try very hard.

I think the bottom line is that corporate America, and corporate Japan, still think of me as someone who can sell a product. I guess people remember me as wholesome and all-American and the girl who won so much at such a young age. A lot of people recognize me walking through shopping malls and airports and usually start staring or pointing. This is when I wish they would come up and say hello. That would make me feel more comfortable. My brother Jeff spends several hours a week just on me, and he represents a lot of tennis players and other athletes. I'm constantly discussing new business options with him, and I'm much more involved in that side of my life now.

For the first time in my life, I've become interested in planning my career and my finances. I know that sounds bizarre, but a professional athlete always has other people to do those things. I have never paid a bill; I've always had financial advisors do it for me. I think most professional athletes have had it that way.

In the last two years, thanks to Scott, I have begun to take an interest in my finances and to develop a system to keep track of them. I have found out exactly how much money I have. I have started to ask questions about investing. I have changed financial advisors. Now I have begun to make my own decisions and take more control of my life.

If you ask nine out of ten professional athletes, they would have no idea how much they have and what is being done with it. They just leave it to agents and financial people to take care of everything from plane reservations to investments to scheduling of commitments.

Well, enough of that for this professional athlete.

When I'm not working my "job," I'm probably working out, doing every stretching exercise imaginable, working on my aerobic conditioning, doing exercises in a pool. My personal trainer, Ken Matsuda, is getting me in shape for . . . well . . . I don't know. Will I come back? I simply don't know.

What am I working toward? We'll see. People always ask me how I think I would do if I were playing now. There's no way to know. If I were coming up now, as a child, I certainly would need more protection. I, too, would develop more of a team, I imagine. Everyone is so sheltered and insulated. When you're a tennis player of the 1990s, you travel with a potpourri of people, including some of the following: parents, siblings, a coach, a trainer, and perhaps even a nutritionist.

I am smaller than some of the women out there, but I certainly would be strong enough to compete with them, especially given the power one can generate with the racquets we use today. I imagine I'd be like Monica, just standing at the baseline knocking the hell out of the ball. I could come back, depending on my knee. If I did, I would have to give up many of the TV assignments and the pro-ams and corporate appearances and focus entirely on tennis, something I have not done since 1989. When I was Number One, I was young and without a boyfriend and totally devoted to tennis. I didn't have many things on my mind except whether to hit the ball cross-court or down the line. The more responsibilities you have, the more diverted your attention becomes. Meanwhile, you have to compete against the kids whose only focus is tennis. That's tough.

I know I've lost some of my intensity. At a corporate clinic in Boca Raton in early 1992, I was playing doubles with Jeanne Evert against Billie Jean King and Ilana Kloss. I hit a swinging volley at Ilana at the net to win a point. Billie Jean glared and I flinched.

"I made Billie Jean mad," I said to Jeanne.

"Are you crazy?" Jeanne said to me. "Chris would have done the same thing."

I think I'm getting soft.

Then again, when I went through newspaper articles and looked at my scores while doing research for this book, it brought back how much I won. Robert Lansdorp told me that watching Michael Chang play is just like watching me play; he's so tough, and when he gets in trouble, he gets tougher. I hear that and I go out and pound more tennis balls.

If I did come back, I think I'd have the ability to reach the top fifteen without much trouble. I will never be able to cover the court as I once did; due to my right knee, I don't think I could ever win a Grand Slam final. Or even be in one. But I do think I could play in the quarters or semis at most tournaments and not be embarrassed.

Another option is coming back and playing doubles again. My leg still has that screw in it and it creaks and hurts often, so doubles would suit me better than singles. It would be fun—but I'm not sure if I'm looking for fun tennis. I have that every day in Los Angeles. I'm wondering about being seriously competitive again.

Having been the best, could I accept just being good? This, I don't know. Since the accident, my mobility has been limited. On days when I'm hitting the ball well, I say, "Sure, why not?" On days when I'm not, I have doubts. I say, "Give it up, get married and have four children."

That is my dilemma. It's not a bad problem to have. I'm not looking for sympathy. I'm a happy person with a lot of opportunities. But I am haunted by the thought that I had to leave the game so young. The last time I played Wimbledon, I was nineteen. Nineteen. When I defaulted in 1983 due to the stress fracture in my back, I was twenty and already starting to do TV commentary. Martina is thirty-five now and still playing. Chris retired at thirty-four. That's thirteen years Chris had that I didn't. I was sidelined at twenty-one but always intended to be back soon at the same level. To see all the talent God gave me go unused troubles me.

During the 1980s, I was going to come back next year, then next year. Who knows what I could have done without the injuries, and then the car crash; in some ways, I feel cheated. I ease that pain by saying I've had a well-balanced life after age twenty-one, which I wouldn't have had if I had been playing on the circuit.

I've never used the R-word: retire. I may never have to. No one thinks I'm going to play again and no one stays up nights wondering about it. Me included. I might be one of the few athletes who left and never came back, but didn't retire.

In fact, I was inducted in 1992 into the International Tennis Hall of Fame in Newport, Rhode Island. What an honor that was; it made me feel, for the first time ever, as if my career was complete. I never thought of entering the Hall of

Fame at twenty-nine. Then again, it seems everything came really early in my life. I didn't expect to play in pro events at fourteen, I didn't expect to win the U.S. Open at sixteen and I didn't expect to be injured at twenty-one. So getting into the Hall of Fame at twenty-nine just completed the circle.

Making it into the Hall of Fame means more to me now than when I first heard the news. At the New York press conference for the announcement, I had to stop talking at one point because I felt tears welling up in my eyes. I was going through my career, reflecting on what I had done and what more I could have done. Could I have won a Wimbledon singles title? How many more times would I have played Martina and Chris? I'm only twenty-nine now, so I would have played Steffi more than the one time I did. I would have played Monica. I would have played in more than one Australian Open and in more than two French Opens.

To have been on top of the sport and then to have been out of it in two years is so difficult for me to think about even now. It would be as if Monica were gone from tennis two years from now.

Now that my peers have retired or are thinking about it, people like John McEnroe and Hana Mandlikova, I'm living vicariously through the process. Reality sets in real quick. Billie Jean King can't stay away from it. She is playing and organizing Team Tennis and doesn't seem to want to stop. It's hard for any top-flight athlete to bury the fire that got them to Number One.

I was reading about Joe Montana a while ago and he said he was a good player in high school, but nobody thought he was great. Now, with his terrific pro career, he has had his greatest success as an adult, when he was most aware of it. I'm so envious of him. For me, it was more like a dream. It would be nice to have some of that incredible success when you're an adult, to be able to understand and be conscious of it.

It also would be nice to leave on your own terms. Kareem Abdul-Jabbar comes to mind; he was forty and decided it was enough. He had played all he wanted. Kareem said in an article: "Jackie Robinson said that every athlete dies twice. But I haven't. I don't miss the game. There was absolutely no sense of discovery there for me anymore. I had achieved more than anyone else. There was nothing left undone."

I will never be able to say that.

Kareem continued: "I know I missed stuff, but I don't know exactly what. For most of my life, I've never lived in the real world."

I also will never be able to say that. Unlike Kareem, I have lived in the real world, or as real as it can get for a pro athlete.

I still have so much energy; call it the impatience of an athlete. I want things now, or yesterday. I want to move from peak to peak, with no valleys. This is why people in Hollywood get so screwed up. It's one high after another. I sometimes ask myself why I didn't try drugs or alcohol. My life left a place for it, yet I never wanted to do it.

I certainly had my weaknesses, but they were more in the area of self-esteem than vices. I wouldn't assert myself to adults. I'd spread myself too thin, always agreeing to play in a pro-am or charity event even when I could use the day off. If the WTA called and wanted me somewhere, I was there. I didn't say *No* enough.

I have become more assertive with my opinions, too. All the TV producers I've worked with have told me to just say what I think, so I do. At Wimbledon last year, a BBC reporter asked me about my injuries and I told him about all those calls from the WTA to play in the tournaments I then pulled out of. When I got off the air, I was told that WTA executive director Gerald Smith was mad at me. "Fine," I said. "Tell him to come and talk to me. He wasn't around then and doesn't know what happened and I'll explain it to him."

Even a few years ago, I would have been scared to death that Gerald Smith was mad at me. Now, I have learned that I have a right to my opinion and I'm confident enough to know that what I have to say is worthwhile. The turning point was when I confronted Pam Shriver at the Open a few years ago concerning her potshots at me. I was proud of myself then and glad I did it. A little self-esteem goes a long way.

I often get asked about "burnout," the catch-phrase for athletes and coaches who have had enough and have to leave their sport. I get these questions because people think it happened to me. I have a three-word answer for that: It did not.

I didn't burn out. I simply couldn't play for five years. I hate it that my name is the first one that comes up when people are discussing burnout. If I burned out and hated tennis, why do I always go to matches? Why do I go to the Volvo tournament? Why do I play so much? Why do I want to report on it for TV? As my old coach Vic Braden says, in a seventeen-thousand-seat arena, if there are three thousand people there watching an exhibition, I will be among them. I am a fan of all sports and go to a half-dozen Lakers and Kings games a year. But tennis still holds the most allure for me. I really love to watch the game and study its strategy.

While I'm rolling, one more thing: in the May 1990 issue of *Tennis* magazine, assistant editor Cindy Hahn wrote a story saying it's bad when juniors play up in age divisions because they don't learn to play with pressure. An example is a fourteen-year-old playing in the eighteens. If he or she wins, great. If they lose, it's OK because they are playing older kids. Hahn wants kids to stay in their age group, play against their peers, and not be pushed too quickly.

As I began reading her article, I found myself nodding my head in agreement. Then, I stopped in my tracks. She quotes Chris Evert as telling me about the merits of age-group play when I was sixteen, with the clear implication I had been someone who had done it wrong. I couldn't believe it because I had done everything right. I won the 12s, 14s, 16s and 18s.

Furthermore, when I was sixteen, I was winning the U.S. Open, so I couldn't avoid playing in the pros. I played in the U.S. Open in 1977, reaching the quarters. And I won the 18s that year. I wasn't hiding out in the 18s; I was looking for competition.

On the subject of journalism: Somebody once wrote that my mother made my dresses. For the next five years, other reporters picked that up and printed it. They made my mother sound like Betsy Ross. My mother doesn't sew—although she did design a line of women's tennis dresses when I was little. I despise lazy journalism.

I always see Andrea Jaeger and me lumped together in stories talking about burnout or tennis injuries or whatever. Yes, we both were injured, but we are two very different people. Our parents are different, our upbringings were different, and our careers were different. I ran into her last Christmas at Aspen, Colorado, while I was on vacation with Scott. We were coming in from the airport when I saw a woman wearing sweats, walking her dogs. She looked familiar. "Wait, that's Andrea," I yelled to Scott. I rolled down the window and shouted her name.

It was Andrea. We chatted for a few minutes, exchanged phone numbers, and ran into each other a few other times that week. She lives up there now; after undergoing at least five operations on her shoulder, she can't play tennis and can't ski. But she seemed very happy, which made me happy. She's almost completely out of tennis now, while I still am playing the game and associated with it. But I find people still mention us in the same breath. It's easy to throw us together and say we "burned out," but it's irritating because once that gets going, it's impossible to stop.

Those are my few complaints. I don't have any more. I'm living a charmed life.

Last fall, I went to Palm Beach, Florida, to conduct a tennis clinic for Pontiac executives. I also gave a speech to about four hundred fifty people. It was quite a day. I was on first, then came Norman Schwarzkopf as the main speaker, followed by singer Lee Greenwood, who finished the evening with his song, "Proud to Be an American." There was not a dry eye in the room.

In my speech, I went through my life with my family, in tennis and now, beyond the game. There were four reasons, I said, why people become successful at anything: desire and drive; discipline to work hard on a consistent basis; belief in yourself; and the ability to dream and set goals.

"Looking back, I feel lucky to have gotten involved in tennis," I told the audience. "My mom loved tennis because it taught us to set goals and gave us something to do to not be diverted to drugs or other areas of trouble. We learned how to win and develop a sense of achievement and we learned how to lose and what could be improved the next time. This is something we could carry on into daily life."

Tennis was not about becoming a professional. "These were social skills for a lifetime," I said. "Hopefully, we would learn how to interact well with other kids and develop good sportsmanship. We gained discipline and confidence that were improving daily. The physical activity was good for us. We learned to respect and take care of our bodies."

My father brought balance to our lives; my mother brought consistency. My dad might not have been as interested in tennis as my mom was, but, I said, "he never had to pay college tuition, due to scholarships and the fact that four out of five of us turned pro. He thanked my mom for starting us."

I went on to say that hard work was the difference for me. Five of my friends at the Kramer Club, including Trey, Anna Maria, and Cecelia, ended up playing on the circuit for some period of time. "Most of my peers were bigger than I was and some were physically more talented, but when I set my mind to something, I'd do it."

Tennis took me places I never imagined. I remember all the good things that began happening. About thirteen years ago, I went to New York for an Avon photo shoot and stayed in a suite at the Plaza Hotel. I told my mom I was going to stay up all night because I had only eight hours in the suite and I wanted to enjoy all of it—dining room, living room, three bathrooms, two bedrooms. Some people never will get to stay in a suite, and I get them all the time. Believe me, I'm grateful.

I arrived in Indonesia once and had my own motorcade to the hotel. I was there for an exhibition with Martina, Kathleen Horvath, and Kathy Jordan in 1983, and ten to twelve cars escorted us. Revlon sponsored the event and gave us facials, make-overs, and massages.

Coming back from Stuttgart one year, I took the Concorde from London to New York. The pilot let me stay in the cockpit while we landed. Adding to my aviation résumé, I recently piloted the Goodyear blimp for a couple minutes over Palm Beach.

I get invited to so many wonderful parties and events that Scott laughingly calls himself "Mr. Guest." Thank goodness he is secure. And has a sense of humor. I need someone who is sensitive and strong at the same time. Scott's good for me. And I think he gets a kick out of this life of mine. He's not afraid to go up and talk to people, whether it's the man running the car wash or George Foreman at an AIDS research benefit.

I am a very fortunate person. But, within my life, there are conflicts and questions and fears. I'm not as good at anything I do today as I was at playing tennis. When you get to be Number One in the world in something, it's hard to let go. It's your security blanket. I've moved into business, motivational speaking, writing, TV broadcasting—and I'm not going to be Number One at any of that. I have to start at the low end of the totem pole. That is so difficult for any athlete, including me, but it's a great challenge.

The one vocation I have found that most reminds me of tennis is television. I like the adrenaline rush of having to perform under pressure—and I like the feeling when you're finished and you've done something you're proud of. I also love the research I have to do for a TV assignment. I enjoyed doing

my homework when I was in school and I love getting prepared for a telecast now. When I do TV work, I'm part of a
team, and I like that. I like working with people who are as
successful in their careers as I was in tennis.

I do know that at some point, I would like to have children. I wonder about Los Angeles in that regard. Sometimes
I think my future husband and I should own a house in L.A.
and also buy a ranch and a lot of land where our future kids
can run. I look forward to slowing down a bit because up
until now, I've lived such a fast-paced life.

I have the same forces tugging at me as do millions of
women in America. I want to have a family like my family.
But I never want to stop working and/or playing. My mom
didn't have a car until her fourth child. Her role was to stay
at home and take care of the kids. I would have to have a
nanny if I kept on traveling, but there's no way then that the
children would be raised the same way I was raised.

As I said in my speech in Palm Beach, "I'm a business-
woman and a TV commentator and I intend to be a good wife
and mother—and none of these rely on a good backhand."

I can't imagine straying far from southern California, because I'm too close to my family to leave them for good. Everyone is nearby except Jeff, who lives in Alexandria, Virginia,
with his wife, Denise, and their child, Kelly, age two. Pam
lives in Redondo Beach, California; John is at PGA West in
Palm Springs, where he lives with his wife, Karen, and has a
son, Christopher, who is eight; and Doug is a real estate developer in southern California. He and his wife, Brooke, have
three children: Brian, eight, Westley, six, and Erin, three.

When we can't find the kids, all we have to do is look for
my dad and the computer. They'll all be gathered around him.

All of us get together at Thanksgiving and Christmas and
play tennis at John's place, even though we're all at different
levels. What else would people expect us to do? What I really
love is when I get to play doubles with my three brothers.

My parents are still in Rolling Hills Estates. My mother

has her daily match at the Kramer Club and my father, now retired, works on his computer and plays tennis now and then. My mom comes over to my house often, if for no other reason than to water my plants when I'm traveling. She still takes me to the airport and picks me up when I return from a trip. Last year, the day after Christmas, she took me to the airport at six in the morning so I could fly to Aspen, then drove home and picked up Jeff and took him to the airport at seven. She just loves to be with her children.

I often reflect on how important my parents have been to me. They gave me my career, they gave me all the values I have. As I said in that speech, "At the end of my life, I will want to have said lots of 'I love yous' and 'I'm sorrys.' I will want to look back to a life full of love, laughs, learning, and trying everything I wanted to do."

When I become impatient, which is often, I think of how it all began, a little girl hitting a tennis ball against the wall at the Kramer Club, then running after the ball and hitting it again.

I still hit a tennis ball against a backboard every now and then.

There are times I think everything has changed. But, in reality, nothing has.

# INDEX